Re-entering

Re-entering

Successful
Back-to-Work Strategies
for Women Seeking
a Fresh Start

Eleanor Berman

Written in Cooperation
with the Ellen Morse Tishman Memorial Seminars
for Re-entering Homemakers, Sponsored by the Hunter College
Career Counseling and Placement Office

Crown Publishers, Inc.   New York

Library of Congress Cataloging in Publication Data
Berman, Eleanor, 1934–
Re-entering.
"Written in cooperation with the Ellen Morse Tishman
Memorial Seminars for Re-entering Homemakers, sponsored
by the Hunter College Career Counseling and Placement
Office."
Bibliography: p.
1. Vocational guidance for women—United States—Ad-
dresses, essays, lectures. I. Title.
HD6058.B525   1980   331.7'02'024042   79-25994
ISBN: 0-517-539438
Design by Camilla Filancia
10 9 8 7 6 5 4 3 2 1
First edition

For F R A N *and* N A N C Y,
who helped me back

Contents

Acknowledgments

I would like to thank the following people who were so generous to me with time, information, and suggestions for additional contacts:

Phyllis Adelberg, Project Re-Entry, Boston, Massachusetts; Marlene Adelman, University of Connecticut; Mary Albro, Smith College; Vilma Allen, Fairfield University; Ellen Anderson, Clairol; Joanne Caulfield, Wider Opportunities for Women, Washington, D.C.; Susan Coffman, New Ways to Work, Palo Alto, California; Helen S. Cooke and Arlene Daniels, Northwestern University; Jack Galub; Marian Goetze, Baltimore New Directions for Women; Sarah Heekin; Judith Hoynes, Vistas for Women, White Plains, New York; Claudette Josephson; Sandra Kahn, Project Re-Entry, Boston, Massachusetts; Muriel Lederer; Regina Logan, Mundelein College; Toma Lord; Wynne Miller, Continuum, Newton, Massachusetts; Donna Nazarro, Fairfield University; Jean O'Barr, Duke University; Ann Orul, Flexible Careers, Chicago, Illinois; Lynn S. Parker, Triton College; Marlene Richman, University of Chicago; Ann Roberts; Katie Ryan, Baltimore New Directions for Women; Helen C. Schwartz; Milo Smith, Displaced Homemakers Center, Oakland, California; Lee Stookey; Madge Tregor, Washington University; Jan Westcott, Drake University; Judy White, Colorado College for Women; Maxine Wineapple, New Options, New York, New York.

A special thank you to Dr. Nancy Stevens and Cindy Friedlander of the Tishman Seminars for their co-operation and invaluable assistance, and to my editor, Marian Behrman, for her unfailing encouragement and many helpful suggestions.

Re-entering

Introduction

Unlike many other books on career planning and job hunting, this volume is directed to a very special audience—the woman who has been or is still raising a family. As a "homemaker," she may have developed many invaluable skills in management, communication, community affairs. But when she approaches the job hunt in the traditional manner, this rich and varied background is often summarized by a prospective employer with an I-see-you-have-no-previous-experience.

The prospect of looking for work raises many questions for this woman. Who is going to want me? What do I have to offer? What can I possibly put down on a résumé when most of my activities have revolved around car pools and the PTA? How will my working affect my family? And even more basic, how on earth do I decide what I want to do in the first place?

Matters are complicated, because the woman re-entering the work scene is often out of touch with many facets of her own personality. Her own needs may have been neglected while she was busy with the needs of her family. And she may be equally out of touch with the exciting new opportunities that are now opening up for women in a great variety of fields.

In short, whether the years at home were three or thirty, whether she has a college degree or not, the notion of re-entering the working world can be a frightening and bewildering one. But armed with the proper preparation, and the techniques especially developed to help women through this challenging time, the re-entry process can become one of the most rewarding experiences in a woman's life. It is a period of exploration, of self-discovery, and of growth, not only for herself but also often for the members of her family who can benefit on many levels from her new role. And it is a role that more and more women are assuming. In 1978, 16.1 million mothers of children under the age of eighteen were at work, an increase of more than 4 million from just eight years before. Widowhood, divorce, the pressures of inflation, and the desire for personal fulfillment continue to swell that number daily.

I undertook a book for these re-entering women with special feeling because I am one of them, a woman who went back to full-time work at the age of thirty-nine. I learned firsthand the trials and ultimate rewards a new career can bring, but I also learned that traditional job-hunting advice is not always applicable for someone who has spent the better part of a decade at home with her children.

A few years later, when an article assignment took me to Hunter College, I became acquainted with the Ellen Morse Tishman Memorial Seminars, a continuing program offered twice each year for women with college degrees and family responsibilities who were thinking of returning to the work force. These women were receiving realistic guidance not only on career direction but also on the personal adjustments the decision to work entails and the fears that must be overcome. They also discussed the mechanics of looking for a job without recent experience, such as résumé writing and interview techniques.

With the co-operation of Dr. Nancy Stevens, head of the Hunter Placement Office and originator of the Tishman program, and Cindy Friedlander, co-ordinator of the Seminars, I have used these sessions as a framework for this book, supplemented by interviews with career counseling professionals all over the country.

Hunter's program is similar to most of the effective career counseling now available for mature women. It helps a woman to assess her skills and put them together in marketable form. There is personal counseling and a unique emphasis on practical career information. Each four-hour session includes a visit from a panel of women working in different fields. They give firsthand insight into what jobs are available. Since many of these women themselves have re-entered the job market after a number of years at home, they are also proof of what can be accomplished in a relatively short span of years as well as a source of honest assessment of what it takes to succeed.

The between-chapter interviews in this book serve the same purpose, illustrating the strategies with which women have forged rewarding new careers in their middle and sometimes even later years—and their feelings about the changes in their lives.

Their stories are important because women need to know that the years spent at home are not wasted and do not rule out career success. Time spent caring for children not only benefits the family but also is often a period of important personal growth. With planning, these years can be used productively by a mother to explore her own talents and interests, to prepare herself for an eventual return not just to a job but also to a rewarding career that uses her own special aptitudes in the best possible way. The earlier the process of career exploration begins, the better the chances of success.

I am grateful to the Hunter staff and to the many other professionals in counseling and education who shared their views and expertise with me. Their efforts and the innovative programs they have begun for re-entering women all over the country have helped to make this a time when a woman can truly look forward to a second focus in her life—a full future rather than an empty nest as children grow up.

Finally, my thanks to the inspiring working women who have contributed to this book, women who have more than compensated for a late start in their careers. They are examples for anyone who is seeking a more fulfilling life-style. They are women who were just starting to work only a few years ago, uncertain of their potential.

If you want to join their ranks, read on.

1. Returning to Work Are You Ready?

If you are thinking about re-entering the job market—or entering for the first time—the first thing you should know is this: You couldn't have picked a better time to start.

Whether you're the occupant of an "empty nest" or a young mother feeling the need for challenge, a former professional or a woman who married right out of school, a woman who wants to augment the family income or a recent divorcée or widow faced with the need to support yourself for the first time, that statement remains true.

Whatever your personal situation or motivation, the climate has never been better for women who are getting a late start in seeking a career. First of all, you're in good company. Millions of women like you are already out there working and their successful re-entry has helped pave the way for you. More and more employers have discovered the value of returning homemakers as workers.

And though finding a really satisfying job is never an easy matter for anyone, the odds are better for you today than ever before because you have more help available than ever before. The nation's educators and career counselors have recognized the need for special attention to the ever-growing number of women who are returning to school and to work. If you are unsure of your direction, there are programs almost everywhere to help you assess your potential and put it to work in the marketplace in the most rewarding way. You'll be learning about many of these programs in the pages ahead.

Furthermore, once you get out there into the wider world, you're going to discover some very nice things about yourself. You can't run a home, raise children, take part in community affairs, be a wife or mother or neighbor without developing a lot of skills in dealing with people, a resourcefulness in solving problems, and a sense of responsibility that are going to help you succeed.

Throughout this book you're going to be reading interviews with many women who have made amazing progress in their careers in a short number of years. You may think "superwoman" when you hear titles such as "vice president," "personnel director," and "assistant district attorney," but they belong to women who were stay-at-home housewives just a very few years ago. These women will tell you they changed once they went to school and to work. They became more confident, more ambitious for themselves. Regardless of the career direction or the level of the job, almost every returning homemaker seems to share in the ego boost that comes with proving yourself outside your own home.

However, most of these women will also tell you readily that they started out with the same insecurities and doubts that you may be feeling right now. Changing their lives has meant giving up some of their old pleasures and making changes at home, none of which came easily. If the notion of working fills you with conflicts and fears, the second thing you need to know is that you are not alone. For many women the obstacles in returning to work are not so much the actual problems of the job market but the personal conflicts that are part of being a woman in an era of changing values.

None of us are immune to these conflicts. We all hear the dual directives that woman today receive—the old message to be a caring, available wife and mother, and the new one, to be an achieving, assertive career woman. Though it is possible to be both, it isn't easy, certainly not at the same time.

Furthermore, it is counter to the role models that most of us grew up with. Even today the majority of new female college graduates grew up in homes where their mothers did not work. And however sincerely we may believe in the benefits of stretching our roles and our definitions of ourselves, however much we may need the stimulation of an outside commitment, we are still necessarily influenced by the only patterns of home life we have known. It is a rare mother who can work without feeling some guilt and ambivalence about her choice and some worry about the effects of her career on her children.

Waiting until the children are in their teens doesn't always work either. Many women have discovered that they still feel the need to concentrate their energies at home just when they had imagined they would feel free to pursue their own goals. One articulate mother who had planned to work sums up the feelings of many women when she comments, "My four teen-age girls' lives have gotten more complex rather than less. While that in itself shouldn't surprise me, what I had somehow failed to anticipate was that it would make them, in some ways, more dependent on us as parents. Five years ago we still made most of the big decisions and the children dealt very competently with the everyday logistics of their relatively simple lives. But now they are very much involved with those things that we once did, or decided, for them, and our supporter/facilitator role seems to take more of our time. Helping is harder than doing.

"While I don't want to be *too* much involved in working these things out, I think there are ways I can be helpful and I want (for my sake as well as theirs) to be available to do that," she says. "And, with four of them at this stage, it's hard to see how I would fit it all into the relatively inflexible schedule of an away-from-home job. I know that others manage to do it but I wish I knew in more detail *how* they do it so that I could weigh the costs and the rewards."

Like so many mothers, this one lacks role models for a changing life-style. She goes on to describe some of the other mixed feelings that come with contemplating a return to work. "I've also been surprised to find that I'm less eager to have a job than I thought I would be. Partly, maybe, because I'm plain *scared* after eighteen years of not having one! And partly it's because I realize there are many things I have time for now, and *like* having time for, that I simply wouldn't be able to do if I had a job. But maybe I'm wrong about that. Maybe the fact that I don't have a lot of free time now (into which I could imagine fitting a job) is the result of some kind of Parkinson's Law that makes things use up more time than they need to. Maybe I'd find, with a job, that I'd use time a lot more efficiently. I guess it's the loss of flexibility, rather than the loss of time, that I worry about with a job," she says, voicing a common concern.

Husbands are another concern for many women who are considering making a major shift in their life patterns. Working means new demands on a woman's time and energy. It must necessarily mean changes in her home routine and in her attitudes. Men, subject to the same kinds of conditioning that prevent women from changing their values easily, need not be male chauvinists to be insecure about the notion of a working wife. Some resent new demands for their participation in home chores and the loss of services they have come to take for granted. Many have sincere worries about the effect of a working mother on their children. And more than one husband secretly worries about what will happen if his wife finds her new life more attractive than the old one.

This whole notion of working women is newer than we realize. It was just 1963 when Betty Friedan's book *The Feminine Mystique* appeared to question out loud the traditional woman's role, and it was at least another decade before the full effect of the women's movement began to be felt. We're all still experiencing growing pains, and neither men nor women have many models to use for a changing way of life. With so much recent emphasis on the emergence of the working woman, it is easy to feel pressured to seek a job before you have resolved the conflicts and adjustments this decision entails.

How to Evaluate Your Options

One of the most valuable things you can do before you begin any search for a job is to try to confront your own mixed feelings, to sort out for yourself which values are truly your own today and which have been imposed on you either by your upbringing or by the pressures of today's society. The old values are the ones that may keep you feeling guilty about leaving your home and children and the full-time role of wife and mother; the new ones can be just as difficult to resist, pushing you to leave home for a job before you are really ready.

Why is it that you want to work? If you need money, of course, that is the most basic and indisputable reason, and it makes any further discussion unnecessary. But sometimes the need for income isn't urgent. Are you planning to work because you feel a deep need for more challenge and stimulation or because it has become the "in" thing to do in your social circle and you're embarrassed to go to another dinner party and admit you do nothing except take care of your home and family? One of the participants in an early discussion at Hunter's Tishman Seminars brought a tremendous laugh of recognition from the group when she told of her feeling of inadequacy at a recent party where she met a woman who was holding down a job, working on her Ph.D., and had just installed a loom in her bathroom.

If *you* are hurrying into the job market because you feel the need for labels or looms to feel good about yourself, stop and consider carefully. Homemaking is a legitimate career, too, an important and demanding one. The real meaning of women's liberation is the freedom to choose the way of life that is most personally satisfying for you. You need to measure your home situation, your energy level, and your priorities before you are ready to establish a plan for work.

When this is done honestly, you may find that a job is not the real answer to your present needs, that a different kind of outlet or solution that leaves more flexibility for home obligations may be what will be best for you and your family at this particular time of your life. Dr. Nancy Stevens, who has helped many women come to terms with their conflicting feelings, states that women who can confidently say they prefer to be at home can feel just as successful as those who decide to pursue a new career. "There are price tags on each decision in terms of sacrifices—your free time, your own values, the impact on your family and marriage. The important thing is to get in touch with your own feelings and do what makes you most comfortable with yourself," she advises.

If this means remaining at home, there is no need to apologize to anyone. You might do well to heed the advice another career counselor, Carol Feit Lane, offers to embarrassed homemakers wondering how to answer when working friends ask how they spend their time. "Tell them you are growing," Ms. Lane suggests.

Often women with family obligations recognize that what is

most practical is a gradual plan to enter the job market in a year or two or five, rather than immediately. This can be a fortunate decision since getting to know yourself and the job market is a job in itself, one that requires time and effort. The more thoroughly you explore and prepare, the greater your chances for finding a career with potential for long-term satisfaction.

Timing your re-entry to minimize its impact on the family helps to keep down the guilt that often comes with taking an outside job. But even after other doubts have been resolved, many women who sincerely want to return to work find themselves with a final stumbling block. Plain and simply, it is fear. The unknown is always intimidating. And society does little to help build confidence for a woman whose main occupation has been her home and family. We tend to ignore the many talents it takes to be an accomplished homemaker, and to overstate the abilities it takes to earn a paycheck. This is compounded because, as women, we are conditioned to be modest about our own accomplishments, to underrate ourselves. The idea of asking someone to hire us for pay brings out all our insecurities.

Some recent studies at the Yale School of Medicine showed that of the women looking for jobs 70 percent were suffering from depressive symptoms and strains so characteristic they could be labeled "job hunter's stomach" and "interview insomnia." What were some of their qualms? Fear of failure. Fear of competition. Fear of rejection. Lack of confidence in their job skills. Fear of having to take tests. All these symptoms tended to disappear within four months after they went to work.

If fear is standing in your way, the only way to fight it is by forcing yourself into motion, beginning the process of changing your life. A constructive start is to take stock of yourself and exactly what you do have to offer, to begin to recognize and believe in your own potential. Just as most career counseling programs do, this book begins with some of the ways you can get to know yourself better—your values, your priorities, your interests, and your talents. This will help you assess whether you are ready to work or to plan for work. You should then be ready to translate what you have learned about yourself into a plan of action, researching where your own abilities best fit into the world of work and what extra job credentials you need to acquire through schooling or doing volunteer work. Then comes the process of job hunting, a less frightening prospect if you do it with careful planning and preparation. And, finally, there is a chapter on sorting things out at home as you begin making your way in your new job.

You can learn a great deal from a book or from anything or anyone who helps you to know yourself better. But self-analysis often becomes more valuable accompanied by some outside evaluation. We are not always able to see ourselves clearly or to do ourselves justice. No book is a full substitute for a good professional counselor when you need one, nor can it give the kind of support and encouragement you may find in a group of women who are sharing the experience of exploring themselves and the working world.

Use this book to get you moving, and as a reference. But do also take advantage of the increasing number of excellent career-planning workshops and courses available all over the country. Note that many of the women interviewed for this book got their first real impetus to re-enter from one of these groups. In the Appendix you will find a listing of career counseling services along with tips for selecting one in your area. You'll also find helpful sources of detailed career and educational information of all kinds and a bibliography for further helpful reading.

Every one of us has untapped potential for learning and growing. Finding a career that is right for you can do far more than add a paycheck to your life. It can do something vital for your self-esteem, your outlook on life, even your appearance. Rather than harming your home relationships, you may find, as many women have, that a career for yourself eventually will revitalize your marriage and improve your relationship with your children. Exposing yourself to new people and ideas and using your abilities in a rewarding way make you a more interesting person—to your family, and even more crucially, to yourself.

We hear a lot, and rightfully so, about the problems and discrimination women continue to face on the job. But we don't hear as much as we should about the tremendous new potential for women today, especially those who would seem to be getting a late start. The women who've agreed to share their experiences here represent scores of others who are more than making up for lost time, moving up in their professions at a pace that would amaze the average worker. They are proving the value of maturity. They are making achievements in fields that were not even a possibility for women just a few years ago. They are going back to school, beginning new careers and new lives at an age when women used to resign themselves to sitting at home and knitting for their grandchildren. They don't tell you that this change was easy or that it does not involve compromises and sacrifices in their lives. They do tell you that the rewards are worth the effort.

It's an exciting time to be a woman, a time when you, too, may become a "late bloomer," making many seemingly impossible dreams come true. It's not too late to start—nor is it too early. The best time to begin is right now, giving some thought as to who you are today and what the right direction is for you.

Rena Bartos

"The years when I was at home were the most rewarding in terms of personal development of any period of my life."

Rena Bartos is one of the best-known women in New York advertising circles. Though her re-entry was easier than that of many women because she was able to return to her original employer, her interview is included here because the comments on what she gained personally and professionally from a ten-year hiatus as full-time wife and mother should interest any woman who feels she has given up her chance for career success by a decision to stay at home.

"When Rena Bartos talks, Madison Avenue listens," proclaimed a recent cover of *Ms.* magazine.

Talk to Rena Bartos, a warm, down-to-earth woman who is a senior vice president and director of communications development for J. Walter Thompson, the world's largest advertising agency, and she will readily remind you that she took ten years out of her career to stay at home, in order to be with her growing son. Were these years detrimental to her professional growth? "The years that I was at home were the most rewarding in terms of personal development of any period of my life," she says with conviction. "Watching a child grow is an education. It takes you out of yourself. Much that goes well in my life today, I attribute to those years."

Rena has become something of a legend in the business, a lady known for her ability to go beyond the stereotypes of market research to see the individuals who make up America's marketplace, especially its female half. Again, she credits her decision to spend time at home with the perspective that has contributed to her success. "If you work and then stay at home, you can quickly learn that people are people, with or without paychecks. Working women are not necessarily more brilliant or better, certainly no more broad-gauged human beings than are women at home. You can't generalize; there's just too much diversity out there."

Interested in the social sciences, but not in teaching or social work, Rena graduated from Rutgers, then did postgraduate work at Columbia University with the late Paul Lazarsfeld, the man who is widely regarded as the father of public-opinion research. She was hired by Lazarsfeld's wife, Herta Herzog, who was involved in the late 1940s at McCann-Erickson, in some of the earliest advertising agency motivational research studies. Rena continued working after her marriage, but though her career was going well there was never a conflict in her mind about working versus family obligations. "I never considered staying on after I had a child," she says. "In fact, I gave notice before I was even positive I was pregnant. And I enjoyed being a homemaker. I became active in my son's school and seriously involved in studying art. I was not discontented and I had no definite plans for returning to work. I did, however, take the occasional free-lance jobs that were offered to me, even though they invariably came at the most inconvenient times. I had a sense it would be good to keep my hand in."

It was on one of those assignments that she bumped into her former employer Herta Herzog, who convinced her that it was time to come out of "retirement." "Herta could charm the birds ouf of the trees," she remembers. "She told me, 'You can be flexible. If you have to be at your child's school, you can say you're at the library.'"

Rena did worry about her son. "I changed the nature of my help at home," she says. "I used to look for people to supplement me. I like to cook, so I never cared about having someone do that for me. Now I hired a more mature, responsible person, someone who could take over the cooking and shopping and offer stability for my son. I also hired a baby-sitter to supplement the housekeeper on her days off. The sitter arrangement lasted for a year before my son announced that he was perfectly capable of being in the house by himself. So *he* fired his sitter."

Coming back to the office required surprisingly little adjustment, she found, since she was returning to the same company and many of her former coworkers. "They had all moved up to management positions, but they accepted me back as though I had never left." And she soon made up for lost time. "I found that maturity was a real advantage in moving up. Coming back, I could see how much the agency functioned just like the PTA. I developed what I call the 'Dr. Spock theory of advertising,'" she says with a grin. "Dealing with many of the more explosive executives is much like talking to a three-year-old with a tantrum. You learn to be calm, consistent, to stand your ground."

In time, she was hired away by J. Walter Thompson to head a new division of creative research. It was here that she made her mark in the industry by being among the first to come up with the notion of exposing agency copywriters to the consumers they were writing for, an idea that was widely copied.

Most recently she has been recognized for pointing out to Madison Avenue that they were underestimating the impact of working women. Not only were half the mothers of school-age children already working, but also half of the stay-at-homes questioned had reported that they *plan* to work. Rena noted from research findings, which had been all but overlooked, that working women had special buying patterns. She noted further that the new "plan to work" homemakers had still other spending patterns and family structures that differed from the traditional homemaker whom advertisers were still trying to reach. Her views on the diversity of today's women at home and at work, the group she calls "the moving target," have been eagerly sought at advertising and marketing conferences and were discussed recently in an article in the *Harvard Business Review.* That article has resulted in a contract to expand the concept into a book, a challenge she looks forward to tackling "though I don't know exactly how I'm going to find the time to do it."

Rena's influence on the advertising world has failed to turn her head. With obvious humor, she describes herself as the "instant expert" whose quotes are being sought on all sides. "It's the advantage of maturity again," she believes. "You can't speak frankly and with conviction when you are twenty years old."

Rena Bartos is a woman who is obviously happy with what life has brought her way. She is still enthused about her work and what lies ahead, pleased and proud to see her son grown and successfully established on his own. She feels her life has been richer because it has had more than one focus. "If you are going to have children, you owe them a good start," she feels. "It's not a sacrifice. And staying at home does not mean you can't come back one day, better for the experience."

Then, in a soft voice, she adds another reason why she feels every woman must make plans for a career as her children grow up, "My husband died suddenly four years ago," she reveals. "Where would I be without my work?"

Betty Hayden

"This was the first time I had ever thought seriously about myself and where I was heading, the first time I realized that I could have input into my future."

Betty Hayden, the traditional wife and mother living in Cedar Rapids, Iowa, three years ago, probably would have laughed if anyone had suggested that she go out to sell business equipment for IBM.

But that's exactly what Betty is doing successfully today. She is a sales representative in St. Louis handling electronic typewriters, copiers, and supplies, a job that sometimes sees her lugging sixty-eight-pound equipment around in order to demonstrate her products.

It's a long way from Cedar Rapids and the days when she says she never thought about taking a job. "Looking back, I guess I was content basking in my husband and children's glory, though I did have rewarding volunteer interests that gave me my own sense of worth. But when my husband was transferred to St. Louis, I wasn't happy about the move. I was leaving my oldest daughter behind in college. I was moving to a much bigger city. As a new volunteer, I wasn't willing to start over again at the bottom. I didn't know what I was going to do with myself, but I knew I had to do *something*!

"Then my husband gave me a birthday present, a course for women at a local college called "Explore." The idea of the course was just what I needed at that time. It was designed to help you decide what you wanted to do with the rest of your life. I was raised in a time when society measured success for a girl in terms of a successful marriage. This was the first time I had ever thought seriously about myself and where I was heading, the first time I realized that I could have input into my future."

Betty's background included a college major in business and experience teaching grade school in the 1950s. "Now I see that selling is a logical combination of those two things. Sales is ninety percent education, educating consumers about how your products can help them. But I wasn't that clear about my objectives when I started out.

"We had been told in our course that one of the best ways to explore careers was to call someone who was doing something that interested you and ask for an interview to learn more about that type of job. I made two exploratory calls. The first was to a woman I had met who worked for the telephone company. She was happy to talk to me and that led to an interview and a series of tests. I knew that one of the tests was a survey of your general knowledge, the same kind they give to high school students applying to college. So I used the students' ACT preparatory handbook to study ahead of time. I became very angry with myself when I realized how little I remembered even about simple arithmetic, how many of my school skills I had lost from never using them.

"Actually the test was not so bad. I did well and was slated for a day of additional testing at their Assessment Center. But before those tests could be scheduled I was offered a position. I had phoned the branch manager of IBM in St. Louis to ask for an exploratory appointment. I got into a conversation with his secretary. It turned out we had gone to the same college. She told me there was a temporary job opening and that I should come in and apply for it.

"That was very good luck, but it could only have happened if I had made the call and made the effort to be friendly. I find in my work, too, that if I can make another person feel comfortable with me, then I feel comfortable, too, and I do better.

"But I do also feel fortunate that the time seems to be right for a woman my age, that society has become more accepting of women returning to work. The job opening was for a marketing support representative. That meant teaching, training people to operate the equipment, and visiting customers to see that our products met their requirements. The manager who interviewed me thought it was terrific that I wanted to begin again at age forty-one. He hired me, and shortly afterward, when that job ended, I was offered a sales position. That meant two months of in-house training, then a month in Dallas, Texas, for intensive training. Frankly, I was frightened of failing, but I don't give up that easily. I did well in Dallas, even received an award.

"Selling is very rewarding and offers me the opportunity to earn an outstanding income, but it is tough. Persistence is a must. You cannot take the first no as the final no. I believe in the quality of the products I market and the method used, the 'needs satisfaction' approach. You listen to your customers, analyze how you can best help to solve their problems and meet their needs. I feel I'm selling productivity and quality, not just a product."

Betty's job has meant a major change in her household. "My husband has been wonderful," she says, "even though he really didn't want me to go back to work. He was happy with the status quo, liked having a clean, orderly, well-run household. And why not? Believe me, I wish I had a wife at home now. He's had to give up a lot, but he understands that I needed to do this.

"The kids still say sometimes they wish I'd stay at home and be a 'real' mother again. But I see how much they've gained in independence because I no longer supervise their complete lives. My second daughter, a high school junior, has become a super cook. When she goes off on a trip she packs her own bags. When my son has an overnight for scouting, he packs his own things, too. Just a couple of years ago I would have done all of that for everyone. They've got to be better off this way.

"Things are bound to give a little at home when you go to work. I'm tired at night, especially at the end of the week. There isn't time to do everything around the house. I liked it better when things ran more smoothly. Given a choice, I would have preferred a part-time job. But I couldn't find anything part time that offered a challenge or that paid enough to make working worthwhile. After all, you give up a lot to work. It *has* to be worth it.

"And I couldn't wait any longer to begin. My youngest child is in sixth grade. Had I waited until he finished school, it would have been too late for me.

"There comes a time when you have to make a decision. Are you going to sit on the sidelines just watching life go by or are you going to give your life some direction? I no longer found it satisfying to stay at home. I can tell you it feels a lot better to be doing something about my life than waiting for something somehow to happen.

"When I finished college I worked to earn money, not because I thought of it as my career. Now I work because I find satisfaction in mastering new skills and meeting new challenges. That makes all the difference."

2. Who Am I?

You're about to become reacquainted with an old friend you haven't had much time for lately: yourself.

If you're like many women, the selfish luxury of time and energy to concentrate on your own hopes and dreams for the future ended when you grew up. As a little girl you were expected to fantasize about becoming a movie star or a ballerina or going to the moon. During the teen years, you probably had some definite goal for yourself, even if it was no more complicated than becoming a wife and mother. Perhaps you also had serious career ambitions when you were in school and worked at them before you had children. But somewhere along the way you became so involved in your many fragmented roles as somebody's wife, mother, housekeeper, and neighbor that you lost sight for a while of any long-range personal goals.

Since no one is likely to get very far in life without deciding where he or she wants to go, some new and definite goals are necessary if you are looking for a constructive new career direction. It's time to get back to that young girl you used to know and see what has become of her over the years, what kind of work might be suitable and meaningful to the grown woman she is today.

It's exciting to take a serious look at yourself once again, but it's also a task that will take time and concentration. It's easy to begin this kind of self-exploration with enthusiasm, then get bogged down again in the thousand and one other demands of your everyday life. Right now is the time to make a commitment to yourself, a promise that you will allot the time needed to plot a new course and follow it through, that you will begin to give priority to your own needs along with those of your family.

Both you and your family members will need to begin to see you as an independent person outside your family role. You may find that a first step toward giving due consideration to your future is to enlist the aid of your husband and children, sharing your new feelings from the very start and asking them to help you as you begin to sort out where you should be going. They are inevitably going to be affected by your decisions. If you make the right choices and become a happier, more fulfilled person, they have a lot to gain right along with you. And while they cannot make your decisions for you, family as well as friends can give you the moral support as well as valuable outside perspective in assessing yourself.

One way your family can begin to help is by keeping you at your task. Set a schedule of exercises and goals for yourself. Ask someone to check on you at a definite time each week to see that your work is done, just the way you've been checking all these years to see that the children have done their homework or your husband has remembered his dental appointment. In this small way, you are beginning to ask your family to recognize that from now on you'll be needing the same kind of support from them that you've been giving out to everyone else all these years.

If your family balks at the idea of seeing you in something more than your old homemaker's role, you may want to bring them in at a slightly later stage, but it is worth a try. You may find that if you begin taking yourself more seriously, others will, too. If the family doesn't prove helpful, try working with a friend. It's particularly beneficial if you know someone who is also planning for work so that you can go through the process together.

Now—with your own determination to see this through and perhaps some friendly help to keep you at it in case you waver—it's time to ask the question: Who am I?

In *What Color Is Your Parachute?* the book that has become the "bible" for career-changers, author Richard Bolles suggests that you begin your self-analysis by writing a complete autobiography of your life. He means a detailed account of all the things that have happened to you, personal as well as professional. If you have the discipline to complete this, it is an excellent way to review your development.

Career counselors have other ways of guiding you to answer this same question. At the Tishman Seminars, women begin by writing down five things they like about themselves. That's harder than it sounds, by the way, since we're all so conditioned to modesty. Try it. Use five adjectives to complete the sentence, "I am . . . "

Some of the adjectives women came up with included innovative, hard-working, fair, generous, calm, open, deep, ambitious, loyal. What about you? Are you understanding? Responsible? Creative? Caring? What are some of the things that are *right* about you?

On to the negative side. That's usually a lot easier. What's wrong with you? Name five things you do not like about yourself. Do it in a positive way, however, by listing things you'd like to change. Do you wish you were better organized? More patient? Less anxious? More decisive? More open? Less procrastinating? Fill in your own blanks.

You can use these lists of likes and dislikes to do another common exercise. Take ten sheets of paper. At the top of each, elaborate on one of the facets you have mentioned, good or bad.

For example: "I am artistic. I have decorated my own home creatively, devised clever Halloween costumes for my children, created booths for the school fair. I like to arrange flowers and design flyers for the organizations I belong to." Or: "I am a procrastinator. I seem to make plans to do things, then get lost in a million other less important projects, never accomplishing the things I want. Because of this I am always making excuses and feeling bad about myself."

In the center of each page, go a step further. Identify two or three needs established as a result of the description you have written, needs that might be job-related, such as: "Since I am happiest when I am allowed the freedom to create, I need an atmosphere where I can express myself artistically in some way. I need a free, nonstructured environment. I need coworkers who appreciate the artistic side of things." Or: "I need to spell out my goals in written form. I need to learn to say 'No' to things that may distract me. I would function best in a structured situation where I don't have the opportunity to wander away from my objectives."

The things you are considering right now may not be new insights, but this is probably the first time you have stopped to take a careful look at yourself and analyze some of the things you need to do the kinds of work you enjoy or become a person you like better.

The final part of this exercise is to try to list at the bottom of each page two things you can do to meet the needs you have noted, long- or short-term. Again, try to relate to a job and be specific. In the case of the artistic woman, her next objective might be research into the kinds of careers that might involve artistic talent without requiring the ability to draw, or to look into vocationally oriented courses that would help her translate her innate abilities into job-related skills.

As for the procrastinator, her immediate plan of action might read this way: "I will set a time limit for something I have been postponing—checking into offerings for adults at local colleges. During the duration of this contract, I will not take on any new projects to distract me. By three months from today, I will make a decision and enroll in at least one course for the fall. If I fail to meet my obligation, I will 'punish' myself by giving up something I really enjoy—playing tennis—until I have fulfilled my contract."

Each of your ten pages will require attention and careful thought. Though the goals are job-related, they must also necessarily affect your overall life-style, as you can see from the case of the procrastinator. When you have completed this exercise, you should have a clearer picture of yourself—what you like, what you want to change, and what some of this may mean in terms of career planning.

At this point you may want to take an overall look at your life as you are living it right now. Draw a circle and divide it into pie-shaped sections representing the way you divide your time in a typical week. Start by making a list of your normal activities, then group them into categories. Some of the categories might be socializing, paid employment, parenting, sports and exercise, hobbies, television, reading, cooking, housework, volunteer activities, carpools, meetings, shopping, eating. Do not include sleep, but do include any other categories that take up your time. Don't forget telephoning.

Almost everyone has a few surprises when their time patterns are spelled out so graphically. If you see that you are putting a disproportionate amount of your time and energy into categories that are not really productive, try the second part of this exercise. Draw another circle and try to set up your ideal time pattern. Add any categories you would like to include, such as work, school, or travel if you need them.

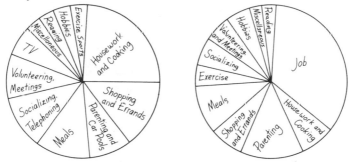

My present time pattern   *My ideal time pattern*

Next, let's see what it would require to change reality so that it is closer to your ideal. Take a sheet of paper and divide it into two columns like the one below:

OBJECTIVE	ACTION NEEDED TO REACH OBJECTIVE
1	
2	
3	
4	
5	

Without stopping to consider what is or is not practical or realistic, begin to fill in the columns. For example, if you want to take a job, you'll have to find time. Suppose you want to cut back on housework. How could you accomplish this? You might hire a housekeeper. Or move to a smaller place. Or divide the chores more equitably with other family members. Or lower your housekeeping standards.

If you want to do more traveling, you may need to provide a baby-sitter to stay with the children, or perhaps send them to a summer camp. That might require additional money. How can you get it? Taking a job might be a solution. Or budgeting more carefully to save toward your goal. Or taking a loan.

Take your time going through this exercise and have a bit of fun with it. Try to imagine just what it would take to change your week from the way it is to the way you'd like it to be. In some areas you may be beginning to see that what sounds like an impossibility may not be quite as far out of reach as you think. There may be a way of getting there. It just involves making some basic changes. And that is the catch. Change seems frightening. But is it really?

Just suppose, for instance, that you did what was necessary to free yourself to take a job and found that you didn't like working? Or weren't successful at it after making all these changes? Well, suppose that did happen. How much worse off would you be than you are right now?

Let's examine some of your fears and see how realistic they really are. Make what is called a "consequence grid." This time you should have three columns across and a line dividing each column in the middle, as below.

Action or Decision	Action or Decision	Action or Decision
Possible Consequences	Possible Consequences	Possible Consequences

At the top of the first column, write the action you might like to take and list below all the possible results you can think of, good and bad. In the second column, put down an alternative course of action, and again, the possible consequences. Do the same for the third column.

If you are considering work, one of the alternatives should be keeping things as they are now, just so you can measure that course against possible changes. You should be able to see clearly that every course has a few negative possibilities. Even if you decide not to take risks, to stay where you are and continue doing the same things you are doing, risk is involved. If you are dissatisfied with things now, you may be unhappy with yourself for not making changes. If your children get older and need you less, you may find you've missed an opportunity to make a better life for yourself. If you should be widowed or divorced or your husband should become ill, if you need supplemental income to send your children to college or to retire comfortably, you may not be able to meet these needs unless you prepare yourself for work.

Something else should be apparent when you measure the consequences of the various decisions you want to make about your life. No alternative is wholly positive, no course of action does not require some amount of compromise. Staying at home may mean postponing or lessening your career ambitions. If you choose to work, you may miss some irreplaceable satisfactions at home. What you must work to achieve is what Hunter's former president, Dr. Jacqueline Wexler, calls "creative compromise"—compromise that allows you to make the most of your situation at every stage of your life, realizing that no decision need be permanent, that we are always free to change and grow as our life situations, our needs, and our values change.

Part of weighing your alternatives means setting up priorities. Which of the possible changes in your life matters most to you right now? Which are possible right now? How much time are you willing to take away from your children? Your home? Your hobbies? How much can be accomplished now by more self-discipline? How many changes will require a period of years to achieve?

There are no right and no wrong answers to your own ideal life plan and no absolute timetable. You must come to terms with your own life situation, weigh what changes are soundest right now, when and how you want to begin them. There's a large difference between procrastination and making a plan for the future. The vital thing you should sense is that you have the ability to make changes to improve yourself and your life, that you may have to make a few compromises with your utopia but that more of it may be within your reach than you might have believed. Where you are headed in the years ahead depends on you. *You* control your future. You can make it what you want it to be. No one can do it for you, but no one can really stop you either, once you have set your priorities and your goals.

Here are two last exercises to help you clarify your overall life goals before you move on to analyzing the specific skills and interests that may determine your career direction.

Pick a time for this first one when you are alone, feeling good about things and with absolutely no distractions. Close your eyes. Imagine it is five years from today. Forget about reality again and try to imagine just how you would like your life to be five years from now. Where are you? What does your home look like? What's the weather like? How are you dressed? Who are you with? It's five years from now, remember. What do your children look like? Go over your day, hour by hour, from the time you wake up until the time you go to bed. This is your ideal day. Let your imagination have full rein. Does it include a job? What kind of job? What do you do all day at your job? This is your fantasy job, just what you want it to be. Are you busy or relaxed, working alone or with others, indoors or out? What kind of work are you doing? And what happens when you leave to come home? How about later on in the evening? No one is going to know about this particular fantasy but you, no censors, no pragmatists allowed. Think hard about it. What would you like your life to be like five years from today?

Now move ahead another five years. Do it all again. Are you still in the same place? The same job? Are the children grown? How do you look? Again, this is your private dream. What do you really want? To escape to a South Sea island, to be president of General Motors? A famous author? A mountain climber? A grandmother? Any or all of the above?

Here's a variation on the same theme. Make a list of all the things you'd like to do before you die—everything you can think of, long- and short-term. Perhaps you want to go to China or learn to paint or speak a foreign language or go back to school. You may have an entirely different set of goals. Maybe you want to lose ten pounds and have a face lift. How many of these things could you accomplish within the next year if you really wanted to badly enough? In the next five years—or ten?

All of this imagining is more than just wishful thinking. How much of your wishes remain just fantasy can be up to you. If you decide what you want and make up your mind to go after it with all the energy and determination you can muster, you can probably go a long way toward making many of your dreams come true —or at least come close enough to make for very meaningful improvement in your life.

That's what this whole chapter has been about, taking a look at yourself and your life, seeing what you do and what you don't like about yourself and your way of living, realizing that all that may stand in the way of making things different is your own lack of direction, your passive acceptance of things whether you like them or not, your fear of change.

Once you decide what you want, you can probably come closer to it than you are today. Creative compromise plays its part. You must be willing to give up some things to gain others. You are going to have to make waves, create change. You're taking risks. It's a bit scary, easier to stay in that familiar rut. But do you want to be there? You can change things if you really want to, can change yourself and the direction of your future.

If you've been sitting back, accepting whatever came your way without much conscious effort at steering a course for yourself, you are going to have to begin taking an active part in setting future directions. The hardest part is taking the first steps, making these first decisions and changes.

And if the course you choose continues to involve finding a satisfying job, broadening your horizons, utilizing your abilities more fully, it's time to move on to the next chapter. Let's examine what accomplishments and skills you've shown in the past that might point the way to the career you should be seeking today.

Michele Rosenberg

"The class was the spark I needed to get me moving."

Michele Orwin Rosenberg is making up for lost time. Director of Public Affairs for a Washington, D.C., research and educational association for the land-development industry, she is responsible for sending out press releases as well as answering media requests for information on almost any facet of the building industry. After a fifteen-month search to find her first job, this is her fourth position in a year in a half—moves that have doubled her salary. "When you start later, you have to move faster to catch up," she believes.

When Michele married after her sophomore year in college, she intended to complete her own degree. "I worked a little, took a few classes—then I became pregnant, and before I knew it there were two children—and that was that as far as college went." She had been at home for six years, reasonably content, when a friend who wanted company coaxed her into taking a career-planning course at George Washington University.

"There were twenty-five of us in that class," Michele recalls. "At the start, the teacher asked how many of us planned to go to work right away. Only one person raised her hand. At the end of the course, there were twenty-five hands in the air for the same question.

"The class was the spark I needed to get me moving. I enrolled in school the week after it ended. The children were just two and a half and five at that time, so I started at night. My husband came home early so that I could leave for class. Then my parents offered to pay for a baby-sitter, and I was able to enroll full time. There was no fooling around this time. I had my degree in five months. As part of the journalism program I took at American University, I interned in a job once a week. That gave me the feeling of what it would be like to be out of the house all day, and it made it easier to think of actually going to work.

"But finding a job wasn't easy. It took fifteen months of knocking on doors. Along the way I did the PTA newsletter and a neighborhood newsletter, anything that would help fill a portfolio and give me something to add to a résumé. I used to walk from office to office with that résumé, looking everywhere for an opening. I no longer had help at that time. When I had a job interview, I had to call on a friend to drive me and to sit with both sets of children in the car until I was finished.

"Right in the middle of this my husband lost his job. I was ready to take anything. But I found that was absolutely the wrong approach. No one seems to want to give you a job because you *need* one. They told me I was overqualified and wouldn't be happy. They asked what I would do if my children got sick. There was a different excuse everywhere."

Like many job-seekers, Michele's eventual success came from someone she didn't even know personally, a friend of a friend, who was director of public affairs for the Civil Aeronautics Board. "I went to see him to ask for referrals to possible openings elsewhere. But he took pity on me. His budget wouldn't allow him to hire me permanently, but he agreed to take me on for six months as a temporary employee. I got the title of writer/editor, a very low rating on the government pay scale, and a low salary to match. Before those six months were up, he had moved to the White House Office of Telecommunications Policy, and he brought me along."

That experience looked good enough on her résumé to earn her a job with the Chamber of Commerce and a substantial pay increase when her six months ran out.

"Meanwhile, I wanted more qualifications, so I went back to school at night to begin working for a master's degree and I began writing free-lance articles," Michele says. Her growing list of credentials allowed her to make two more rapid job changes, adding up to a very respectable salary at last, more than double what she had started with.

"But it was more than money that kept me moving," she notes. "It's hard being a grown-up and having to do the beginner jobs that usually go to much younger people right out of school. I had more life experience and I found the lower-level jobs difficult to accept."

Because Michele had been at home during those "first three

years" said to be crucial to a child's development, she feels that some of the guilt she might have felt about going to work was eased. "I wouldn't have thought of working then. I felt I was the best person to be with the children during those early years. I was the person who cared the most about them," she states.

But though her children can hardly remember the time when she was at home, they are still vocal in letting her know they would prefer her to be there. "They'd like *me* to take the job our housekeeper has," she says with a smile. "We sit down and talk about this frequently, about why I need to work away from home. I try to explain that I needed to get out, need something to occupy my mind. I wasn't very creative about amusing myself at home. I never even joined the tennis games most of my friends enjoyed. When I was with the children all day, I found myself looking for anything to keep them amused and out of my hair. That's not what I call being a wonderful, creative mother. I appreciate them more now, and because of that I think I'm a better mother."

Michele feels that going to work has had a positive effect on her marriage. "My husband is relieved that I don't look to him to provide my entertainment or my contact with the outside world anymore. Oh, sure our dinners are not what they used to be, and he sometimes has to take a turn going to school conferences now. But my salary is not just pin money for us. I make almost as much as my husband today. My car and my household help come out of my own salary. If my husband were totally supporting me, I might have settled for less money and a more satisfying job. It was financial need that led me into public relations rather than the editing and writing I would prefer to be doing. But I hope some-day to get to the point where I can afford to move into that area.

"The course at George Washington was invaluable to me in giving me a framework for evaluating my needs and future goals. We did a lot of reading about life options, learned to think of our lives in terms of the next forty years, not just next year. I realized that I have a lifetime of being employable ahead of me, and that knowledge made a great difference in my outlook.

"In my case, and for many other women in that course, it was not a new career direction that emerged, but a return to the course I had planned when I started college. My original instincts about wanting journalism as a career were correct, and they still apply today. The difference in looking at my career from the perspective of a thirty-two-year-old instead of a twenty-year-old is that I know now how important it is to be responsible about money, as well."

One of the greatest problems for women, Michele believes, is that "we are so isolated into groups of other women just like us. Most of my suburban neighbors don't work. Most of the women I work with don't have children. We don't have enough opportunity to learn from the experience of others what we can do with our lives. It's one of the things that makes it harder for a woman who has been at home.

"The one piece of advice I would offer to a woman who is re-entering the job market or beginning late is to realize you can't stand still waiting for the perfect job. You take what comes, learn from it, and move on and up as quickly as you can. I still hope to find something more satisfying and with less stringent demands on my time, but getting started has given me the confidence to know that if I have to have a job, I can do it. That makes all the difference."

Annie Fox

"Succeeding in my work has been such a positive reinforcement."

Annie Fox will proudly show you her distinctive business card, printed on green-lined mock ledger paper, lettered "Debits and Credits." At age fifty-nine, when some people are beginning to plan for retirement, Annie launched her own business. Her story of late-in-life professional success is a happy one, and it is hard to believe this slim, energetic, and enthusiastic woman when she tells you that ten years ago she was a very retiring housewife.

Though she had kept the books for her husband's business, Annie had not worked outside her home for thirty-two years when she decided it was time to look for a job. "My husband had sold the business, the children were all gone, I just didn't have enough to do," she explains.

"But the prospect of job-hunting at age fifty-three was a little scary, and I decided to test out the market a little bit. I signed up with an office temp agency and spent about a year sampling different kinds of companies in the area. That experience taught me a great deal—mostly about what I *didn't* want in a job. I saw that I would not be happy in a big company where I would be doing the same mechanical job all day. I was happier in smaller places where there was more diversity to the job and I could work to my maximum.

"When I felt I had gained enough confidence about what was happening in offices today, I began telling everyone I was looking for a job. By good luck, my husband's accountant knew someone who needed some part-time help with the books for a small manufacturing company. I started there and it grew into a full-time job. I spent five happy years there until the company was bought out by a larger firm and the nature of my work changed. Now I was back to the very kind of detail work I didn't like. I was working for a big company. I wanted to make a change."

After she had returned to work, Annie began to regret the fact that she had no college and no official accounting credentials. "I wasn't sure at the start whether I would stick it out for a degree, but I did begin taking courses at night at the local community college. I was very encouraged when I learned I could earn credits by taking the CLEP [College Level Examination Program] exams in English and accounting. My life experience was enough to pass those easily and I immediately had a twelve-credit head start. So I continued taking a couple of courses each semester, and in about three years I finally had my associate degree in accounting."

Annie recalls with pleasure the telephone call she got from the college shortly before graduation asking if she would be attending the class awards dinner. "I had no intention of going, of course. Then they told me I was getting an award as top student in the class. I couldn't believe it. I had been a good student in school years ago, but we had no money for college. Now after all these years, I had finally done it—and gotten an award to boot. What a feeling!"

What did it feel like returning to school after so many years? "At the start I felt like everyone's mother, frankly. And some of the courses required seemed like a waste of time—business math was something I had been doing for years. But there were some really exciting teachers. And the kids turned out to be very friendly. They accepted me, called me by my first name. At the end of my economics course the professor made me feel very good by telling me that I had been a valuable addition to his class. What made me feel even better was having him add that one of the students had commented on how glad he was that I was there, because the practical questions I asked were often things he wanted to ask, too, but didn't have the nerve. My maturity had actually benefited the class, it seemed."

With a degree to bolster her confidence, Annie got the inspiration for going into the accounting business for herself when she saw a friend successfully launch a temporary employment firm. "She had already referred two small accounts to me as extra ' moonlight ' business, and now she became a third. Since accounting is work I can do at home, there was a relatively small investment to try it on my own—just stationery and supplies, a good calculator, an extra business phone, and a listing. I decided I would give it a year. If I could earn a living, fine. If not, I decided I would consolidate whatever accounts I had on a free-lance basis and take on an additional part-time job. Within six months I had already equaled my former income."

She built her business by visiting large accounting firms and letting them know she was available for smaller clients. She offered employment agencies a "finder's fee" for new referrals. She got work by word-of-mouth referral from her accounts—and two new clients from an ad in the telephone book. The business came so fast, it became a problem.

"I found I had to limit new accounts for a while and work out a more efficient system—for myself and for the input from my clients. Eventually I was able to streamline things and take on more clients. But soon I was back to the same dilemma. I had to make a decision as to how big I wanted to grow, whether I wanted to hire a staff, or whether I wanted to take on only what I could personally handle with some occasional part-time help for detail work or typing. I decided that I was going to cut off at my present seventeen accounts and leave time for some flexibility in my life. After all, that was one of the reasons I had decided to go into business for myself. Being able to set my own hours had been a major attraction of being on my own."

Her business success has done a great deal to make her a happier, more self-confident person, Annie states with conviction. "I was neither adventuresome nor confident during my younger years. I believe my personal growth began about ten years ago when my son went into therapy. Through that crisis, I learned a great deal about myself, and my values and priorities began to change. I am a different person today. I'm much more outgoing. Where I used to be timid about talking to strangers, now I enjoy meeting new people. I've gained enormously in my personal relations because succeeding in my work has been such a positive reinforcement."

The "new" Annie has fulfilled many of the wishful dreams she did nothing about in her earlier years. "I always longed to travel, but my husband was not interested so I stayed at home. Now I've been to Europe, Israel, and the western United States on my own. I even went river-rafting in Colorado.

"The one negative of owning my own business is that I can no longer take long periods of time away from home. A week's vacation is about all I can manage. But that hasn't proved serious. As a result, I've just discovered many interesting places close to home. Day by day, my hours are my own. I can take time to spend an afternoon with my daughter or to play tennis. All in all, life is very good."

3. What Can I Do?

Some people call it a "success pattern." Others talk about "significant achievements." Whatever the terminology, current career counseling for adults is usually based on an assumption that seems to work for almost everyone. The assumption is that each of us has an optimum way of operating that brings out the best in us and that if we look into the past to recognize that pattern of operation, it will dictate our best direction for success in the future.

Helen Cooke, alumni placement consultant at Northwestern University, who frequently counsels adult jobseekers, calls these past events "peak experiences," those that used the particular skills and gave the particular rewards that give you peak satisfaction. "If you can analyze what it was about those experiences that was satisfying and see what they all had in common, you will begin to understand what is most likely to motivate you to succeed," she suggests. "Skills are only one part of it. They are not enough without motivation. I see many people with sales ability, for example, who would never succeed in that field because they have negative feelings about selling. Each of us responds to a different set of rewards. Each person has to find the key to the personal motivation that triggers his or her best efforts."

So sorting out your past achievements is a two-part process. First you must consider what kinds of things you do best, your top abilities. Then you will evaluate which of these things you enjoy doing most—and why. The activities that combine your skills with your maximum motivation will constitute your own success pattern. There is usually a recognizable pattern all the way back to childhood.

Often women who have not worked outside their homes for a while blanch at the mention of work skills, feeling they have none to offer. But the very activities that have occupied you at home, given a different set of titles, are often those that have value in the marketplace. Manager, purchasing agent, administrator, teacher, counselor, fund-raiser, landscaper, seamstress, decorator—you have probably been all of these and more. Let's look back at your achievements throughout your life with an eye to picking out job-related skills. The process can be broken down into a series of steps.

Step One: Significant Achievements List

Begin by dividing your life into manageable small segments, starting with the earliest period you can remember. For most people, that means elementary school. Some find it works best to group events in five-year periods; others find it easier to remember things according to specific life experiences such as high school, college, first job, marriage, motherhood, etc. Try them out and choose the way that works best for you. If you took the time to write an autobiography earlier, use it now to help jog your memory.

To list these achievements, you'll need a chart like the one that follows. First fill in dates and achievements, then go back to analyze the skills it took to accomplish each listing. Next, consider the kinds of satisfactions you gained.

Remember, you are looking for achievements that were significant to you personally, events that gave you a good feeling of pride and success. These need not be accomplishments that were major in the eyes of the rest of the world. It only matters that they were important to you. Women at the Tishman Seminars wrote down everything from appearing in a school play to being invited to the junior prom, from getting a first job to redesigning a kitchen to volunteer activities in the community. Some remembered with pride things they had created or repaired; others tended to think more in terms of events they had planned or managed. The chart you make should look something like this sample, and it may run for several pages before you are through:

Time	Achievement	Actual Work Required	Skills Used	Rewards
1974–75	Chaired citywide program for foreign exchange students	Screened applicants Recruited local host families Arranged transportation Organized corps of local student sponsors Counseled students Arranged social events for students and host families	Judgment of people Organization Management Selling Advising Co-ordinating Supervising Promoting Hostessing	New friends among host families Gratitude from students Satisfaction at success of project Recognition from write-up in local paper Contact with diverse cultures Contact with young people

The skills you list should be in terms of active verbs so that they will be transferable to your résumé eventually. Some of the verbs that may be appropriate include:

read	co-ordinate	contribute	label
write	calculate	co-operate	interview
explain	encourage	manage	locate
interpret	counsel	discuss	map
apply	anticipate	draw	mark
edit	appraise	estimate	match
choose	assemble	explain	question
abstract	arrange	find	measure
plan	serve	formulate	modify
organize	set up	generate	operate
persuade	categorize	graph	order
speak	change	identify	outline
memorize	sell	budget	participate
perform	chart	illustrate	prepare
collect	classify	delegate	record
create	choose	improve	reorganize
initiate	recognize	increase	report
communicate	define	interact	respond
research	demonstrate	interpret	revise
analyze	design	itemize	select
decide	compile	decide	predict
solve	construct	join	monitor
promote	transfer	elicit	locate
simplify	translate	detail	tabulate
speak	use	entertain	inspire
summarize	verify	teach	repair

This is one exercise where group interaction is extremely valuable because you probably tend to underrate your own achievements. Mastering French or gourmet cooking, putting together an art show or a rummage sale, solving a local school problem, or tutoring disadvantaged children are some of the activities that are often mentioned almost apologetically by the women who performed them, but that are seen as far more significant by other people. The reinforcement that comes from positive feedback on your accomplishments does a lot for your ego and may even suggest promising directions you have missed in your own evalu-

DEMONSTRATED SKILLS	Achievements	Student	Editor	Cheerleader	School officer	Copywriter	Decorator	Flower Arranger	Photographer	Writer	Administrator	Points
Read		x	x		x					x	x	5
Write		x	x		x					x		4
Explain		x			x					x	x	4
Interpret		◢	x		x				◢	x	x	8
Edit			x								x	2
Choose			x									1
Plan			◢					◢		x	x	6
Organize			x							x	◢	3
Persuade			x	x	■					x	x	8
Speak				◢						x		3
Memorize	■											3
Perform				■								3
Create			x		x	◢	x	◢	■		x	10
Initiate			x		x	x				x	x	5
Communicate		x	x		x	x			◢		x	7
Arrange artistically						■	■	■				9
Analyze			x			x				x	x	4
Problem-solve		x	x			x				x	x	4
Make decisions			x		x					x	x	4
Co-ordinate			■								■	6

ations. If you can't join a group, ask close friends or family to help you examine your achievements in terms of the skills they reveal. Even on your own, if you view yourself objectively, you should be able to see that you have done things that were meaningful to you at the different stages of your life, and you can now begin to sort them out a bit.

Step Two: Top Ten Achievements

With your long list in hand, go back and select from the achievement column the ten achievements that you consider most significant. It doesn't matter when they occurred in your life, only that they continue to seem important to you today. These are the building blocks you will work with to get a clearer fix on your working goals.

First you will analyze these achievements strictly in terms of skills. Make a new chart like the one on the opposite page: achievements across the top, demonstrated skills listed down the side. In each appropriate column, put a check for each skill used. Now go back and pick out the one skill you consider most important in successfully carrying out this activity. Blacken that square. Select the second most vital skill involved and fill in half of that square. Time to tally the score. Count three points for each black square, two points for the half-filled squares, and one point for each check. You should come out with three or more skills that stand out and a few others that rank as close contenders.

Tests that measure career-related interests usually divide them into six categories. They are (1) physical and mechanical skills, (2) problem-solving and analyzing, (3) helping people, (4) detail work, (5) leadership, and (6) originality, creativity. Though this is far from a scientific measure, looking at your skills should give you an idea of patterns. Where do you seem to fit in? Which categories seem strongest? Do you seem best with people, data or things?

Right now you should take a separate piece of paper, which will serve as your worksheet, and begin to assemble some information

for later use. Label it: Ideal Job Description Data. Put down your
top skills and the two interest categories you've noted above:

```
┌─────────────────────────────────────────────────────────┐
│ I D E A L   J O B   D E S C R I P T I O N   D A T A      │
├─────────────────────────────────────────────────────────┤
│ Skills:   Create                                          │
│           Persuade                                        │
│           Interpret                                       │
│                                                           │
│ Career interests:   Originality, creativity               │
│                     Leadership                            │
│                                                           │
│                                                           │
│                                                           │
│                                                           │
│                                                           │
│                                                           │
└─────────────────────────────────────────────────────────┘
```

You'll continue to add to the sheet as you collect more information about yourself. Meanwhile, back to your top ten achievements.

Step Three: Personal Characteristics

The purpose of this exercise is to help you recognize some of the
personal qualities that affect your working aptitudes. List your
achievements once again across the top of the chart, but instead
of skills, the following list of demonstrated personal characteristics will go down the side. Put a check in each achievement
column where the quality seems to apply. Give each check one
point and select the three qualities that seem to stand out to be
added to your job description sheet. This list has been adapted
from exercises commonly used by career counselors. If some of
your most significant personal qualities seem to be missing, add
them to the column.

DEMONSTRATED PERSONAL CHARACTERISTICS	Achievements											Points
Adventuresome												
Ambitious												
Analytical												
Cheerful												
Competitive												
Considerate												
Courageous												
Creative												
Friendly, outgoing												
Helpful												
Honest												
Independent												
Intelligent												
Logical												
Obedient												
Patient												
Persistent												
Physically attractive												
Responsible												
Sensitive												

Step Four: Work Satisfactions

Here you will examine the last element in identifying your success patterns, motivation. Begin by going through this list of reasons why a person might find a particular job satisfying. Rate these for yourself, giving three points to your most important considerations, two for moderately important, and one point for those that matter least to you:

_____ Chance to help society as a whole
_____ Chance to help other people individually
_____ Chance to meet new people
_____ Opportunity to be part of a team
_____ Opportunity to exercise leadership
_____ Can prove my competence
_____ Can assume responsibility, make decisions
_____ Pushes me to operate at a high energy level
_____ Does not pressure me with deadlines or competition
_____ Gives me recognition
_____ Exercises my reasoning faculties and problem-solving ability
_____ Shows immediate results of my efforts
_____ Allows me to create order, set up systems
_____ Involves social status and prestige
_____ Offers variety, change
_____ Allows for creativity and originality
_____ Provides strong supervision
_____ Allows for independence
_____ Chance to learn and grow
_____ Uses my precision skills with data or things
_____ Offers stability, security
_____ Uses my social skills
_____ Provides me with an audience
_____ Offers a high earning potential
_____ Challenges my abilities
_____ Involves a field that interests me

It's interesting at this point to compare the rewards you have given high marks to those you listed as part of your significant achievements. If the correlation is not high, you may want to think about how honest you are being about your motivations. It may sound good to say you want to "help people" but in reality you may derive more satisfaction from managing them or from analyzing data or doing precision work. If you are conditioned to think that your values should fit along traditionally female, unselfish lines, you may be automatically limiting yourself to the kinds of jobs that have been considered proper for women in the past. Teaching, social work, nursing, and counseling, all fine "helping professions" that have attracted women, are also fields that tend to be crowded and low-paying. It's just as valid to want a high salary as it is to want to be of service to others. There's nothing shameful about wanting recognition for your work or doing the kinds of things that are most satisfying to you. Don't limit yourself to motives you think you *should* want. Be honest about what rewards really give you most pleasure. Look over your top-rated categories, pick the three that seem most important to you, and add them to your worksheet.

Step Five: What, Where, Why

You will add two optional listings to your worksheet here. First, if you have a particular area of interest so strong that you might like to make it a career, note it here. That might be sports, music, architecture, sewing, science, business—whatever turns you on.

Then think about the kind of working conditions you would prefer. What is more appealing to you, small and informal or large and structured? Indoors or outdoors? A small shop or a tall sky-scraper? If you have a strong preference, note where you think you would most happily spend your time day after day.

Step Six: The Ideal Job Description

You have a worksheet now that lists three skills, two work categories where you seem to fit, three personal characteristics that you've demonstrated as valuable on the job, and three rewards that motivate you. You've added appropriate notes on your special interests and the atmosphere you'd prefer on the job. Now your goal is to combine these into a short model job description, a paragraph that tells what your job would involve if you could tailor a position to your own exact specifications.

Never mind if you think your dream job doesn't exist. Like looking at your life goals, this exercise is intended to give you something to work toward. Try to describe a job that would use your top skills, offer the kind of coworkers and working conditions you would like to have around you, result in something you consider rewarding. You may even be able to condense your description into a want ad. "Situation wanted: Position requiring organized, responsible person with proven ability to motivate others. Duties to include heavy contact with people, planning and co-ordinating activities. Small, community-oriented office, non-profit organization preferred." Or perhaps: "Position desired for persistent, detail-oriented worker skilled at setting up systems, organizing data. Work to include analyzing, problem-solving. Prefer large, prestigious company with room for advancement, chance for recognition."

Each person's want ads will be slightly different. And just as an employer often has to choose among several promising applicants for a job opening, you will likely find that there are several career choices that might answer most of your needs. The first ad, for instance, might be answered by someone seeking a public relations worker, a department supervisor, or a fund-raiser. The second could well fit a systems or sales analyst, a computer programmer, or an accountant.

To give you some ideas of the variety of careers that involve many of the same skills, here is a listing the University of Michigan offers its graduates suggesting possible career paths for an English major:

correspondent	insurance underwriter
community organizer	personnel worker
copywriter	public relations
editor	publishing
lawyer	scriptwriter
library work	reporter
management trainee	technical writer
writer	teacher

All of these careers, some seemingly totally unrelated, involve the ability to communicate clearly in writing and/or an interest in literature. If writing were one of your chief skills, these are all potential career areas that might utilize your talents. In order to make a decision as to which you'd prefer, you would have to learn more about the total content of each job and the work environment, the other skills that must be combined with the ability to write.

Here's another example of the same principle. Students in a vocational counseling class at Hunter came up with a list of 179 occupations that involve counseling, from advising on financial investments to dealing with drug addicts. The settings of each job, the additional skills and knowledge needed to perform it well, vary enormously.

Good counselors and good salespeople are both involved with listening and diagnosing needs. Similarly, lawyers and computer programmers both must analyze and set up strategies to solve problems.

You've determined some of the important elements your ideal job would include based on what has comprised your most satisfying achievements in the past and your present values and interests. To use this information most meaningfully, you must now turn to analyzing the world of work more knowledgeably, looking carefully at the opportunities and options for putting your particular assets to work in the most rewarding way.

Most people, even working people, have limited knowledge of what various occupations entail in the way of daily duties and skills. Before you actually seek a job, your goal should be to explore what people actually do all day in the jobs that might be right for you, particularly in some of the less traditional fields that offer special opportunities for women today.

Phyllis Needy

"How could I sell myself to an employer when I didn't know what a job was?"

It had been twenty-one years since Phyllis Needy earned a paycheck, and her first problem in looking for a job was a very basic one. "How could I sell myself to an employer," she asked, "when I didn't know what a job was? I had no idea what people in different occupations did all day."

As it turned out, it was her own search for information about the job market that eventually led to a satisfying new career for Phyllis. Five years ago she became a program co-ordinator at the University of Washington Placement Center in Seattle, counseling women, as well as graduates of both sexes of the schools of business and economics, on the realities of looking for work. The path to that position, however, was a long and sometimes frustrating one.

"I graduated from Stanford in 1949," Phyllis relates, "found a job almost by accident as the assistant director of a children's museum in California, and stayed just two years until I got married. Then I spent a year as a receptionist for a group of physicians, got pregnant, and that was the end of my early 'career.' Nor did I have regrets. I was happy as a wife and mother and busy with many rewarding community activities, particularly as part of a docent program at the Seattle Zoo, where I trained volunteers to give talks to schoolchildren and added many new directions to the project."

By the time one child had entered college and the second was about to follow, however, it became obvious that extra income would be welcome to help with tuition bills. So, at age forty-five, Phyllis began to consider finding paid employment.

"I started reading ads," she recalls. "When I saw one that sounded appropriate with the local Head Start program, I just went right over to apply. That's where I realized how unprepared I was to look for work. I couldn't even fill out the application properly. I didn't have names of references and had to write 'deceased' in order to get around providing addresses for former employers. I went home to 'regroup' and get together the information I needed even to apply for a job.

"When one of the local department stores advertised for Christmas sales help, I went down mainly to prove to myself that I could do the application right this time. As it happened, the personnel director came along while I was there, talked to me, and told me to come down for the training class beginning the next week. Some of my friends couldn't understand why I was taking a job as a salesperson, but I felt I needed to do that. I needed to start at something where I could learn what it meant to work and, more importantly, some place where I could succeed.

"A paid job is not the same as being a volunteer. As a volunteer you are welcomed and praised. As an employee, it is taken for granted that you will do your job. I needed the discipline of reporting on time, staying all day, and following orders.

"It takes hard work to succeed at anything," Phyllis observes. "They assigned me to the luggage department. Before I was through, I had learned a lot about luggage as well as about management, because, when I was alone on the floor, that department was my responsibility. After the season, it made me feel really good to be offered a permanent job.

"But it wasn't what I really wanted to do, so I began doing more investigating. I went to the University of Washington to find out about getting an advanced degree. There I met the head of Woman's Programs and discussed with her my own difficulties in finding a career direction. As a result of that conversation, a class was designed for women like me who needed to explore the working world—and I was hired to lead the group. The intention was to answer the questions I had asked myself: What do different jobs actually entail? How do I match my own skills with the requirements of a paid position? We sent class members out with a letter of introduction to local employers where they gathered this kind of information. We compiled files of job descriptions and learned the kind of vocabulary that was proper for writing a résumé. So much of business jargon is really a kind of vocabulary matching game, and women have to learn how to play."

As they interviewed, the women were also finding potential

slots for the internship program that the university was operating under a federal grant. The internships were designed to allow women to learn on the job. Just at that time the grants director retired, and Phyllis was appointed to the position of coordinator for the remaining year of the grant.

"During that year I also began interviewing for other jobs—and getting turned down. I was passed over because of my age, my lack of business skills or experience. I spent six months pounding the pavements, concentrating on finding my "niche." But in spite of the rejections, I began to feel better about myself and my abilities. I saw realistically that my best chances were in education or social agencies where my age was not necessarily a disadvantage. I was forming a clearer idea of what I could get and also of what I wanted. I was learning how to present myself.

"When an opening came up in the college placement office, I applied in spite of the fact that they preferred someone with a master's degree. I was able to convince them that the practicalities and problems of finding a job were much the same for college graduates and for returning women because neither really understands the realities of the job market—and that I could be particularly helpful because of my own experience. I was very happy to get the job, and I love what I do. In addition to helping students, I've been able to reach out to women in the community in many ways."

Because of her own background, Phyllis has much to say to women who are returning to work today. "Don't be afraid to try a job at the bottom to learn what working is all about," she advises. "You should not be influenced by what other people think or by titles. There's a necessary learning period when you go to work. Part of what you must learn is humility, something that is difficult when you have been the boss in your own home for many years. I feel it is more important to start where you will succeed than to jump into a higher-level spot where you may be programming yourself to fail.

"Someone once said rightly that there are no dead-end jobs, only dead-end people. You need not stay where the opportunity for growth is limited, but you can learn from every experience."

You are responsible for recognizing what the situation is and taking appropriate action—which may mean changing jobs.

She also cautions women not to look at a job as an escape from problems at home. "A job is not a magic answer to anything," she observes. "If you have felt trapped at home, you may feel trapped in a job. Wherever you are, it is up to you to create positive satisfactions in your life, to find opportunities to grow. No one can do that for you. Instead of sitting back waiting for the world to do something for you, you must take charge and take responsibility for the quality of your own life."

Neither Phyllis nor her husband had fully anticipated the changes a job would entail at home. "When my husband encouraged me to find work, we never stopped to think of the compromises this would mean for him. It has taken great patience on his part to adjust. While women are finding new directions, we need to bring men along in the process," she believes. "I see many women here in Seattle supporting one another in their efforts to change their lives. Men need their own support systems to learn to accept this."

With tuition money as her prime motive for working, Phyllis expected to quit when her children were finished with college. Now, at age fifty-three, she is committed to her career.

"My early years at home were rewarding and valuable and I wouldn't trade them for anything," she states with conviction. "But these years are important to me because I have proven myself outside and am doing something that is personally satisfying because it uses my skills in a meaningful way. I wouldn't even want to predict what I'll be doing five years from now," says this woman who didn't know how to look for any job just a few years ago. "I wouldn't close off anything or limit myself. Life is too full of possibilities."

Helen Stuart

"I've changed and grown tremendously."

"When I look back, I see myself standing at the picture window of our home, looking out, waiting—always waiting—for my husband or my daughters to come home."

Today Helen Stuart looks out from the thirty-fourth floor of an office skyscraper, though the hectic pace of an advertising account executive's day leaves her little time for gazing at skylines. Her re-entry job at age thirty-nine: secretary.

"As I moved into my late thirties, I recognized that things were happening to me that I didn't like," she says. "I had two bright, rebellious daughters. I began to feel that I was instigating some of that rebellion because I was looking for my self-identity through them. I was triggering problems because I didn't have enough of a life of my own.

"The girls were twelve and fifteen, in school all day and busy afterwards. We had recently moved and I felt few ties to my new house or new community. I was feeling defensive, put upon by my kids and by my husband, who all seemed to consider me a depository for problems and dirty laundry.

"My husband is a scientist. He has a job with a great deal of prestige, but not a matching salary. He was constantly being invited to conferences all over the world, but there was never enough money for me to go along. One day I watched him on his way out the door to a meeting in Moscow. I was obviously unhappy to be left behind. He looked back at me and said, "When you can pay your own plane fare, you can come, too." That was it. I made up my mind to get a job and make enough to pay my own way.

"But I had no thought of doing anything beyond being a secretary. That was frightening enough. I hadn't worked in fifteen years and then only at secretarial jobs. I was terrified just at the prospect of filling out forms and taking tests to apply for any job."

Helen knew that she wanted to work close enough to get home

in case of an emergency, and that she preferred a large company. "I was just curious to see what went on in a big corporation," she says. "So the logical place to go in my area was General Foods, which fit both categories. I didn't try to con anyone there about my qualifications. This was fifteen years ago, before so many people went back to work. I told them that I felt my assets were reliability, the ability to take responsibility, and to deal with people. I also told them quite honestly that, while my children were normally quite self-sufficient, in an emergency I would put them first. They were taking a chance on me. The man who hired me was younger than I was, and that was most unusual. But they decided to give me a try. Most of my coworkers at my own level were twenty and twenty-two years old. It was several years before I moved to my own age group and these were women who had been there for years. It was awkward.

"One day soon after I began, my boss was telling me about his major marketing project, a new dog food. He described his target consumer—a woman in her thirties with a house in the suburbs, two kids, two cars, and a dog. It hit both of us at the same time. He was describing *me*. So he began trying out his ideas on me, using me as a kind of in-house consumer research package. The marketing people began to consider my feedback valuable, and my own self-esteem began to grow. And I advanced, level by level. About that time, the company hired its very first female M.B.A. for its training program—that's how different things were just a decade ago. I had become an administrative assistant to a divisional business manager. We used to discuss how many talented women in the company were being underutilized. I had been there for seven years by then—and I was going to be offered a junior-executive position. It was a real breakthrough. And then we moved away.

"In a sense, I was re-entering all over again, but I had a different sense of myself this time. I had worked with many advertising agencies while I was at General Foods and I was interested in that field. We knew someone who had a small agency, and he asked me to become his administrative assistant, but I said 'No thanks.' I wasn't going back to that. Then he offered me a deal. He needed help. He promised that if I would work for him for one year, he would give me the chance during that time to learn the workings of the entire agency. I agreed and he kept his word. At the end of the year, I hired a new assistant for him and I became an account executive. Unfortunately, the agency had financial difficulties a few years later and was forced to close, but by then I had my credentials and was able to find a responsible job."

Looking back, Helen regrets that she did not begin working sooner. "I've changed and grown tremendously because of working," she observes. "I was not ambitious when I was young, had no career goals, didn't finish college. Advertising is a field that stresses youth, and I've felt that my age was a disadvantage in moving into positions of really senior responsibility that I would like to have today.

"Of course, hindsight is easy. I don't know how I would have come to terms with the guilt if I had gone to work when the children were younger. I do know that my working has done wonders for my relationship with my family. My daughters are on their own now, and our communication has never been better. They're just amazed at my language and attitudes. I have to keep up—it's part of my job. I have to know the terminology young people are using, the current trends. At one point when I first came to this agency I was involved with the introduction of a new motor bike. The president of the company was in his thirties, the vice president in his twenties, and I was past forty. Yet we got along. They had respect for my background and my life experience, and I was able to communicate with them in their own terms. I know that I am more informed, more up to date, more involved, and surely more interesting because of my job.

"For the most part, my husband has been helpful. My working posed certain problems for him. He was forced to change his patterns at home, become more supportive of my needs. I make more demands on him, he must be more independent. Today I think he is a little bit awed by my responsibilities and the money I bring in. But my salary has enabled us to enjoy a better life-style and he appreciates that. He realizes that, in a sense, he has to pay for this life-style by giving up some of the things I used to do for him at home. Our relationship is different—and I believe it is healthier.

"It took me a long time to get where I am because I wasn't directed enough when I went back to work. I wasn't aware of the broad spectrum of jobs and opportunities out there, or of which skills are marketable. A good account executive, for instance, has mediator instincts and communication skills, must be the middle man between the creative departments and the clients. Account executives also are co-ordinators—they have the ability to go out and find specialists, to fill needs, put the parts together. Many women possess these skills. But they must add the final prerequisite, a knowledge of marketing.

"I'd advise a woman starting out to shop around through courses, to talk to people in the fields that interest you, to learn what you need in skills and credentials to move into a field. Then, use any contact, any means to get in the door."

Advertising is a demanding profession in terms of time and personal energy. Helen Stuart enjoys some of the pressures of her job, and it gives her the wherewithal to travel almost anywhere she might want to go today. But like many successful executives, she has discovered one of life's ironies: She can afford the plane tickets to travel now—but not the time.

4. Looking at the Possibilities

Now that you have a more definite notion of the kind of work you'd like to be doing, where are you most likely to find it? If your fields of interest already have become clear to you, skip ahead at this point. But suppose you are not sure of your targets just yet —or don't feel you have enough knowledge about the job market to make an informed choice. You need an overview of the job market as a whole as well as some more concrete information on the work involved in different types of occupations before you proceed.

One of the handicaps facing women who have had limited recent work experience is that their knowledge of the possibilities is limited to what is familiar. Name the jobs whose functions you know best. Chances are they are the kinds of "helper" positions mentioned in the last chapter, those traditional female bastions of teaching, social work, counseling, nursing, and secretarial work.

But where are the best opportunities for women? According to a policy proposal recently submitted to the U.S. Select Committee on Aging, "the best economic opportunities for midlife women are in nontraditional careers, contrary to the early socialization they received . . . higher-paying careers such as electronics, crafts, sales . . . rather than such traditional overcrowded and low-paying fields as teaching and nursing. Fund-raising and public relations, which build on the experiences many women gain in volunteer work, are fields in which women do particularly well," the report notes, while in spite of their typical math anxiety and fear of things financial, "knowledge of math-related fields such as budgeting, finance, and accounting is an important skill that can enhance women's opportunities for better careers and improve control of their personal financial lives . . .

"Although some professional careers are largely foreclosed to midlife women because extensive graduate education is necessary," it continues, "many nontraditional careers requiring much less training offer realistic opportunities . . . such as nuclear medicine technology, medical records technology, respiratory therapy, computer science, and health safety."

These are among the fields you might investigate before you make a final career decision. And they are only the start of some of the exciting opportunities just opening up. You've only to check your daily newspaper to pick out some other promising possibilities. A recent item in the *Chicago Tribune* stated, "A shift from oil and coal use to solar energy by 1990 would create almost three million jobs for Americans." If you are concerned about the size of your fuel and gasoline bills and want to become educated about the alternate uses of solar energy—or almost any matter having to do with energy, for that matter—you can probably have your pick of good jobs.

Read further in the papers. Two-paycheck American families are eating out more and spending more money for leisure activities and travel. That means jobs are increasing in resort, hotel, and restaurant management.

We're growing older as a nation, so there will be more jobs in gerontology, health care, and hospital administration. Urban affairs, industrial security, grants management, and fire-protection engineering are examples of promising new career areas that have emerged only in recent years. Computers have only begun the revolution that continues to open up jobs for people who are equipped to enter the electronic data fields. Women are finding new chances for advancement in industries such as insurance and banking thanks to new equal-opportunity laws that affect their employers. And we've all read about these new "managerial women" who are climbing slowly but surely up the corporate ladders of many kinds of businesses.

There's a whole new world out there for you, and even if you finally decide that the more traditional areas are where you want to be, you owe it to yourself to explore the possibilities, to look into some of the less traditional ways in which you may be able to put your skills to work pleasurably and profitably.

In order to determine which of these fields might be realistic for file of career information. Some, like Chicago's Flexible Careers and California's Woman's Way, actually have a library of taped interviews with women working in a wide range of jobs so that you can hear firsthand what their daily work is like and the opportunities that exist in their fields. The Catalyst publications, which you'll find in most libraries and career centers, are other good sources of information on specific occupations.

Through your research, you want to find the following things:

What are the various job categories in this field?
What do these jobs entail on a daily basis?
What are the usual entry-level positions?
What preparation is required to qualify?
What are the usual paths of advancement? Salary prospects?
What are the future prospects of the industry?

Let's take just one sample industry, insurance, and consider what you might learn from some careful reading. First, what is this business all about? People buy insurance as protection against the financial uncertainties of life. They purchase policies, paying a relatively small amount of money into a common fund, thus entering into a co-operative risk-sharing plan to guard against relatively large losses in case of accident, theft, ill health, or untimely death in the family. It is the business of the insurance company to design and price its policies and invest the premiums received so that there is always enough cash on hand to cover customers' claims as well as enough left over to insure a profit for the business. You're probably aware of this—but what does it mean to you in terms of possible jobs? Here are some of the unique positions within the insurance field, determined by the specialized structure and aims of this type of business:

Actuary: Studies statistics on births, deaths, marriages, employment, retirement, accidents, etc., to determine premium rates that will be both competitive and profitable for the company. Skilled actuaries are in heavy demand. Beginning qualifications are usually a degree in math or business or economics, including study in calculus, probability, and statistics. Professional advancement comes from passing standardized examinations while on the job.

you in terms of the preparation required and right for you in light of your own aptitudes, you'll need to invest time in research. You might begin with what is often called "stimulus response," an exercise designed to widen your exposure to the myriad jobs that are available. Judith Hoynes of Vistas for Women, in White Plains, New York, suggests that her clients read the want ads in a major nearby metropolitan Sunday paper—all of the ads—and note any of the listings that appeal in any way. She, and other counselors, send people to the library to seek out the *Dictionary of Occupational Titles,* the massive volume published by the U.S. Department of Labor that lists more than thirty-five thousand job titles. When you skim this tome, don't screen out anything because it seems unsuitable or silly. Put down every title that intrigues you for any reason, anything you might conceivably want to do. When you look over your list, you may see patterns that will indicate some job areas that might not have occurred to you.

The next place to go for preliminary job research is the U.S. government's *Occupational Outlook Handbook.* This details some seven hundred occupations grouped into thirteen overall categories, tells you the nature of the jobs in each, the training required, the probable earnings, and the outlook for the future as far as job opportunities are concerned.

From the woman's point of view, one of the best books around for sampling a variety of vocational areas is *I Can Be Anything,* by Joyce Slayton Mitchell, written with new graduates in mind but packed with concise information about jobs in more than a hundred fields and how they rate for women. Another good book directed to women is *1001 Job Ideas for Today's Woman* by Ruth Lembeck. In addition to detailing a wide selection of occupations, it contains ideas on part-time, free-lance, and at-home jobs.

With these survey volumes as a start, hone in on three specific fields that seem worth exploring in further detail, and head back to the library for books in these areas. In addition to the books and pamphlets available at the library, check the listings in the back of this book for the wealth of free information available from professional organizations in every field. You'll find that many college vocational offices and career guidance centers also keep a

Underwriter: Approves policy application and decides whether extra premium is needed to cover greater-than-normal risk. Most underwriters have college degrees but some high school graduates are hired as underwriting clerks and work their way up through on-the-job training. It is a job that involves exercising judgment, assuming responsibility, and making decisions.

Claims administrator: Responsible for verifying claims in order to approve payment. Requires attention to detail, a good memory, an understanding of people, some math ability, but no special background or education. Training is provided.

Investment analyst: Selects the areas in which the company invests its money. Usually requires strength in analysis and evaluation, a college degree in economics, finance, or commerce. Since a company's investment decisions are influenced by social and political changes, people with a combined interest in economics and political science would be especially well suited for this career.

Insurance agent: Actually an independent business person who sells and services the company's policies. Requires understanding of sound financial planning, ability to communicate well with people. Companies provide extensive training during a period of paid employment, then agents work on commission. Women agents are in demand, particularly to service the growing number of women who are assuming responsibility for their own finances.

In addition to these specialized occupations, insurance companies employ accounting and data-processing staff, personnel administrators, librarians, advertising and public-relations specialists, lawyers, and large clerical and maintenance staffs.

What else should you know about this industry? It is not a "glamour" field, does not pay particularly high salaries, but does offer the opportunity for extensive on-the-job training, excellent fringe benefits (especially when it comes to insurance), and is a secure, relatively recession proof industry. And since most insurance companies are federal contractors, they are being forced to make more management opportunities available to women as part of their equal-opportunity program. At New York Life Insurance Company alone, the number of women in management has increased from 25 to 114 in the past 10 years.

This is the kind of basic overview you should be able to gain from reading about any field that interests you. But reading is only the first part of exploring in terms of your own potential. Let's assume you think you might be interested in becoming an insurance underwriter, that the requirements seem to fit your set of special skills. How do you find out more about what this job entails in terms of day-to-day settlements or what the atmosphere is like in an insurance company? The simplest, most direct way is to talk to someone who is presently engaged in this occupation. First, try to think of someone you know or know about through friends or relatives, who works in an insurance company. Try local counseling services or your college alumni office for possible lists of resources. If you can't come up with anyone, just pick up the telephone, call the nearest large insurance company, and ask to speak to one of their underwriters. You're going to ask whether he or she can spare a few minutes to talk with you about the job, explaining that you are interested in this as a possible future career. Remember to stress that you are not asking this person for a job. At this point you are not even positive that this is the job you want. You are asking for the chance to learn firsthand about the work.

You'll be pleased to find that most people seem to respond to this kind of request with enthusiasm, happy to talk about their work, and somewhat flattered to be asked. If you are a bit shy about calling out of the blue, tell your "role model" you are part of a group exploring career options just as the Tishman Seminar participants did. In fact, if you are part of a career planning group or have friends who are also looking into work opportunities, doing this as a group project saves much time and duplicate effort.

If you happen upon someone who is less than accommodating to your request, don't be put off. Just try someone else. If your first interview seems promising, visit more than one company in the field if possible, getting a feel for the different kinds of working atmospheres you might encounter with different employers. Here is a list of questions Hunter suggests when visiting someone who works in a field of your interest:

1. What do you do in your job?
2. What do you like about your job?
3. What do you dislike about your job?

4. Please describe what you did yesterday in detail; for example:
   What was the first thing you did?
   How long did that take you?
   What did you do next?, etc.
5. Was this a typical day? If not, how did it differ from a typical day?
6. Of all your various duties, which ones occupy the largest share of your time?
7. What advice would you give to anyone who wants to do what you are doing?
8. What are the salary ranges for jobs in your field?
9. What was your preparation for this job?
10. Would you suggest the same preparation today or are there additional requirements now?
11. What are the advantages and disadvantages of your occupation?
12. Are there any questions I should have asked you that I did not ask you?

If you are considering professions such as public relations or sales, which can span many fields, it is almost essential to find out what this type of job is like in a variety of settings. Though basic skills such as writing and communicating verbally may cut across all areas, doing public relations work for a small nonprofit community organization is quite different from what is required to publicize and create good will for a national company or a product. Selling, too, varies enormously according to the product involved and selling life insurance to individuals might require an entirely different set of techniques and knowledge from selling health-insurance plans to a large company. One might be quite compatible with your interests; another might turn you off. Selling is one nontraditional profession for women worth investigating because it offers entrée to a number of fields and is a career with high earning potential. David King, codirector of an agency that specializes in recruiting women for executive sales, pointed out to the Tishman Seminars that intelligence, verbal and social skills, and good character, strong assets for a successful salesperson, are skills that many women possess. He also stressed that no degree or special experience is necessary and that many companies offer exceptional training opportunities for their sales forces.

If you have interest in a career in math or science, and need contact with women who are presently involved in these fields, the Math/Science Resource Center at Mills College in Oakland, California, may be able to help you. The center, which has a particular interest in re-entering women and is planning a re-entry program for women in computer science, sponsors informational workshops and maintains a network of more than three hundred professional women involved in areas such as biology, chemistry, astronomy, and engineering.

For information on starting your own business, you can get guidance and probably resource referrals from the nearest office of the Small Business Administration. Of all endeavors, this one bears most careful research. If you talk to a businesswoman like Sue Freehling, who presides over the Freehling Pot and Pan Company in Chicago's Hyde Park, you'll learn that it has taken her 2½ years to turn a profit. Sue opened on a minimum budget using savings. To live off the store immediately would have required a $150,000 to $200,000 investment, she estimates. "It takes patience, hard work, and luck to make a go of a business. You can't help but learn from your mistakes—they sit on the shelf and stare at you. You have to think it out, have a definite goal, keep at it, and not get terrified. It takes time. And the demands of a store have to take precedence over other aspects of your life. It's a real commitment."

Some women have a different kind of exploration to do at this stage of career planning. Suppose you aren't interested in traditional business. Suppose you have a special talent or avocation, something you like doing so much you'd like to turn it into a business. Suppose you really love to cook, for example, and know that you have a special knack for it. What can you do with this kind of skill?

Lots of women have begun food-related careers right in their own kitchens by marketing their own specialties. Rose Totino was a midwestern homemaker with a special pizza recipe that became so popular that Rose is now a vice president of Pillsbury, the company that distributes her frozen pizzas across the country. Two friends in New England have set up a profitable service providing gourmet box lunches for meetings. They sell to everyone from church auxiliaries to business seminars. One Texas lady set up her own rolling taco stand on the streets of New York and was so successful that a customer decided to loan her financial backing for a restaurant. Two Connecticut homemakers are successfully marketing their own homemade Italian sauces, freezing and packing them in plastic containers for local specialty shops. The options are many, and they are not always laid out as neatly as jobs within a company. Your research here might be analyzing what people like and need and can't find readily in the way of food. You can learn a lot by getting out and talking to caterers, restaurateurs, and food retailers in your community, who know the local market as well as the realities of the food business. They may know of people who've tried ideas similar to what you think you might like to do.

If you really love cooking, you might even consider training to become a chef. The *New York Times* carried a continuing saga for a while of one woman who got a job in a suburban restaurant kitchen when her stockbroker husband found himself short of customers during the last recession. She worked her way up through soups and salads to main courses, and learned so well that she eventually became a head chef.

With additional schooling you might consider careers in home economics, as a dietician or food scientist, in company test kitchens or acting as a food stylist whose job it is to pretty up dishes for photographs. And don't overlook your neighborhood McDonald's or Burger King. They are always looking for supervisory personnel and offer extensive management training.

Cooking is not the only traditional homemaking skill that can be converted into a profitable career. The Innovative Sewing Workshop in Edmonds, Washington, just outside Seattle, was opened recently by two women who learned their trade during their years as wives and mothers. Partner Sara Wolters says she has been sewing "ever since my mother thought I was old enough to work the machine." Her talent stood her in good stead when her diplomat-husband's career took the family to Africa for nine years. "You couldn't buy ready-made clothes, couldn't even buy patterns," she recalls. "So I learned to make patterns from our own clothes and then to design my own."

Her designing flair began to bring requests for her services from other diplomatic and Foreign Service personnel in the area, and when the Wolters returned to Seattle, Sara did sewing in her own home. Then came a divorce and the need to augment her income. She went to the Individual Development Center in Seattle for counseling, seeking guidance in marketing her skills in the most profitable way. "They gave me the support I needed so badly during this difficult period," she says gratefully. "And the testing and counseling showed me I had the organizational and management potential to take on a business of my own. Sometimes you need someone else to point out that many of the skills you acquired at home and accept as routine are valuable to the outside world."

With a coworker she had met while working in a Seattle store, Sara came up with the idea of the Innovative Sewing Workshop, which offers custom dressmaking and designing, sewing classes, alterations, and consultations for women who want advice on putting their wardrobes together. The response has been positive from the start, and Sara feels confident about the future. "I wasn't afraid to go into business," she says, "because I know the skills we have to offer are hard to find. There is very little available between ready-made clothing, which is often poorly made and fits improperly, and extremely expensive custom clothes. We fill a real need in the middle for many women—and even men come in for suits because they can't be fitted properly in the stores."

Equally important, Sara feels extremely happy and fulfilled in her new business. "I love it," she says with obvious sincerity.

Cooking and sewing are obvious avenues for some women, but you never know where you may wind up if you begin putting your own special abilities to work commercially. Jettie Yeckley of Birmingham, Alabama, has formed a flourishing business supplying and caring for indoor plants for area businesses. At the end of this chapter, you will read about Ann Cole, an Illinois mother whose creativity with crafts and games has moved her into a dozen exciting and challenging directions.

If your need for a job is not immediate, there is still another way to test out a selection of careers before you make an ultimate commitment in terms of job search or education. It's something you've probably been doing for years without ever thinking about it in terms of career potential. Volunteering has long given women the opportunity to expand their skills and knowledge and it can be used selectively to find out whether a particular field is right for you as well as to acquire working credentials. Many women have discovered this almost by accident. Irene Elders is a perfect example of someone who discovered unexpected skills and a new career as a volunteer. A youthful grandmother who had never worked for pay, her talents were at crafts—or so she thought. Accepting an invitation to teach weaving at her city's senior citizens center as a volunteer, Irene found that she had an unusual knack for working with the elderly. She gained enormous satisfaction in teaching new skills to older persons, had infinite patience and empathy with their limitations. Soon she became more involved in the center, helping to plan a better-rounded program of activities. When a job came up as part-time assistant to the director, it was offered to Irene.

Once again she learned that she had untapped potential, this time as an administrator. A year later the director moved away and Irene took over the reins of the center with no difficulty at all. Without a college degree, she was handling a job whose requirements for an outside applicant would have been a master's degree in social work. Some years later, when her own husband retired and the Elders moved to Vermont, Irene's work experience at the center qualified her for a responsible position with the state Department of Aging.

The list of women who have carved careers from their volunteer experience could go on and on: a faithful Friend of the Library who became the paid public-relations director, a long-time hospital volunteer who was hired as the paid assistant director of volunteers, a member of the board of directors of a city housing authority whose increasing knowledge in her field led to a job as assistant to the authority director. You may be able to parlay your past experience into a paying position right now, or to use volunteering to acquire experience in a field of your interest. If you want to obtain job skills, however, don't settle for routine jobs stuffing envelopes and making phone calls. Plan your volunteer work meaningfully in terms of future career goals. Pushing a hospital cart is not a transferable job skill. Public relations, fund-raising, and staff work experience are what you need, wherever you choose to give your time. Think in terms of a résumé. Have a focus. Don't give up your interests, but combine them with valid job experience.

Wherever you choose to volunteer, ask for responsibility, show sufficient interest and initiative to make yourself valuable, and be sure to keep records and samples of your work for future job-hunting use. You can't expect every volunteer job to turn into a paid position, of course, but if you are serious about learning, you can add many skills to your résumé this way as well as pick up invaluable work references.

You may also be able to use volunteering to help you get ahead in your chosen field. Sue Isaacs, a woman who returned to school for a master's degree in teaching children with reading disabilities, planned her course of study over a period of years while her own children were young. During these years she supplemented her courses with carefully selected volunteering, researching a variety of possible future job settings. She worked in special schools, in special-education classes in the public schools, in private schools, and in clinics, learning how different organizations employed their special reading personnel and weighing where and how she worked best with youngsters. Eventually she found a slot in her own children's school where, as a volunteer, she was able to see that the gifted children needed special reading attention along with those who had special difficulties. Her innovative double-target program was so successful it was adopted as part of the school curriculum, and when Sue earned her degree, she became a paid staff member in the job she had created for herself.

Recently the idea of volunteering has spread from its traditional nonprofit setting into business. It isn't really such a new idea, since apprentices who work in exchange for the chance to learn a trade have been with us for centuries, and many students intern while they are in school. But the notion of allowing mature women to learn on the job is a new one and is spreading rapidly. Some of the structured internship programs available will be discussed in the next chapter, "Going Back to School." But you can also do some job researching and testing on your own by offering your services for a limited time in return for the chance to gain experience and knowledge in a particular area.

Lenore Freeman, who was interested in learning what was involved in career counseling, offered her services at the University of Florida in Gainesville and was readily taken on as an intern in the Career Resource Center. Betsy Laverne was able to convince her local shoppers' newspaper in Connecticut to let her do feature writing as an intern, giving her services in return for the chance to accumulate a portfolio of published articles. Both these women, if they are happy with their choices after experiencing the realities of working in the field, have beaten the old catch-22 of job-hunting—no way to be hired without experience, no way to get experience without being hired.

At some point during all of this exploring, something should have clicked. You should have developed a deeper interest in one of the fields you have explored, an intuition that this could be the right place for you. You have a direction at last, a goal to aim for in that vast job market.

It may also well be that your research has told you that more credentials and specialized knowledge are needed to qualify you for the field you want, and this may mean contemplating a return to school.

That in itself can be a frightening prospect if you've been away from formal education for many years. But things have changed on the campus. There are lots of older students just like you out there today—a third of the total enrollment, in fact. And the nation's colleges have geared up and changed in many ways to better serve these returning students.

Let's take time here to look at some of the varied educational opportunities available to mature women today.

Ann Cole

"What it really takes most of all is energy, the energy to go after what you want and make it happen.

Parents in Ann Cole's neighborhood in Winnetka, Illinois, usually knew where to look if their children were missing. Most of the time the kids could be found sitting around the table in the Coles' kitchen, happily involved in one of Ann's games or crafts projects.

"I laugh when I think about that," says Ann. "My kitchen was really my living laboratory."

Today Ann has turned her creativity with children into a unique and satisfying career. Her company, Parents As Resources, was a pioneer in recognizing the importance of parent involvement in early childhood education. Through activity books and workshops, PAR helps parents gain the skills and confidence to work with their young children.

"I began to realize that what came naturally to me did not come so easily to many other parents," Ann relates. "My own friends seemed to feel uncreative with their children. They were always asking me, 'How do you always know what to do with the kids?'

"Then one day I was a hostess at a training session for Head Start teachers and I realized that the concerns of those parents and my suburban neighbors were similar. Both needed to learn how to help their children learn, to share experiences, explore, communicate, and have fun together. I began to think if I could put my ideas on paper, parents could use them to begin working with their own children."

Ann had graduated with a teaching degree, but she had never actually taught because she had her first child three days after graduation. "I was so pregnant I was embarrassed to march with the graduating class," she remembers with a grin. Three more children followed in the next seven years and she was still very much a busy stay-at-home mother when, at age thirty, she decided to tackle a book.

"With so many demands at home, I didn't think I could handle it myself," she relates, "so I found three partners, a former teacher and pediatric social worker among them. Together we divided the activities according to the preschool curriculum so that the book could be used to supplement children's classroom work. We pooled ideas from our own childhood, our own children, from research, and from brainstorming. We tried things out on our own children, but we also wanted this book to be workable for inner-city parents. With not much more than enthusiasm to recommend us, we went to Chicago Head Start to ask if some of their parents would be willing to test our activities with their children. I still marvel that they said 'Yes.' I guess we had a funny kind of credibility—we had no formal sponsors, no ulterior motives, didn't want money for our time. They agreed to help.

"The only way to show these parents what to do with their kids was to literally sit down in a group and "play" together. As a result, the parents gained a new understanding of what their youngsters could learn from play. More important, a special kind of fellowship emerged. They began to feel comfortable together, able to open up about their problems at home. We saw that this activity approach was fantastically successful. That's what we have been using for the past ten years, structuring activities to meet the needs of the particular group we are working with.

"We made a three-page outline of what we could do in the future with this idea, listing every possible way to reach parents. It's incredible to look back and see how many of those things we have actually accomplished."

Finding a publisher for the book was No. 1 on the list. While the search went on, the women began publishing copies themselves, using handprint on sheets of colored paper. A report on their project in a national magazine brought twenty-five hundred orders for the book and a major mailing operation in the Cole home. "I set out all the pages and the kids would walk around the dining room table collating them," says Ann of their early publishing venture. "The children and their friends helped clear the recreation room and set up a 'map' of the United States on the floor in order to sort our orders by zip codes. Talk about a living geography lesson!"

It was one of these handmade editions that found a publisher. It crossed in the mails with a rejection letter from Little, Brown. "When the publishers saw our colorful illustrated book rather than a typed manuscript, they changed their minds and offered us a contract," Ann relates. *I Saw a Purple Cow* came out in 1972 and has sold more than one hundred thousand copies. Two other books have followed, and a fourth and fifth will be published this year.

Meanwhile, the women found a more professional way to produce their own inexpensive publications, calling them *Recipes for Fun*. There are four in the series now, one printed in Spanish. There has also been a TV series for parents and a syndicated newspaper column. Ann's particular interest has been in PARs training workshops.

"Our first workshops were for women who ran day-care centers in their own homes," she says. "Then a small foundation grant enabled us to set up leadership training programs for parents from preschool centers around the city. In each case, the participants in our sessions returned to offer workshops to parents in their own neighborhoods. Our aim was a chain reaction, developing parent leaders who could teach other parents.

"The most far-reaching project we have undertaken was a three-year pilot funded by the Chicago Department of Health working with parents and children in neighborhood public health clinic waiting rooms. It was a new way to reach inner-city families. We trained teams of workers and were able to handle two hundred and fifty families a week in six different clinics. We learned so much," she happily reports, "did so much good, trained people, provided jobs and information, developed leadership, gave impetus and confidence to parents as well as providing a friendly ear for their concerns."

Ann will deliver a paper on this program at a national conference of the Association for Care of Children in Hospitals. It is one of scores of speeches and workshops she and her partners have given in the past several years in thirty-six states. Their audiences have included teachers, children's librarians, home economists, doctors, nurses, social-service workers, teen-agers, and parents.

"I've gone into many of these things feeling a little terrified," she confesses. "One thing just continues to lead to another. When I began finding myself speaking to Ph.D.s and M.D.s, I was so nervous I couldn't eat, was almost sick to my stomach in fact. But I've learned to take it in stride. I've learned a lot about myself, that I actually do best when I need to extend myself to meet new challenges, and that careful preparedness is the key to confidence.

"And I've found that my own enthusiasm and belief in what I do are infectious, that I have the ability to reach the average parent whether in a Chicago housing project, a Hawaiian Head Start center, or a hamlet in the Appalachians. I've never gotten over being excited at seeing other parents get excited about what their kids are doing."

Ann admits that her increasing involvement in her work has given her occasional qualms about giving enough time to her own children. The guilt has been manageable, she feels, because she was at home during the early years, which she considers so crucial to a child's development. "And the children have always been a part of my work, have helped and tested things for me. Right now my twelve-year-old helps with editing. They do resent it when I am away a lot but I've tried to keep the traveling down to short, widely spaced trips. When I must be away, I believe that my oldest daughter feels good about my willingness to trust her to take over the household. The important thing is that I feel I am a better parent because I am stimulated by what I am doing."

She notes emphatically that her career would not have been possible without her husband's support and understanding. "He had to adjust to a total change in my roles from homemaker and volunteer to a person running a business, traveling, and meeting publishers' deadlines. It is not easy to make that change in the middle of a marriage. It takes a lot of work and communication and constant compromise. Working has meant a tremendous drain on my energy trying to manage both career and family, and at times each role has suffered some neglect because of the other.

"But I can honestly say that I can't think of a single day I haven't enjoyed in the past ten years. I've written, taught, traveled, consulted, trained. I'm constantly meeting new people and discovering new ideas. Every day is different and exciting. I get calls and letters from all over the city, all over the country. I never know what the next day will bring.

"I think my experience ought to show every woman that anything is possible if you believe in what you are doing and are willing to work hard and be alert to opportunities when they present themselves. I never could have foreseen where that first book would lead. You must be slightly aggressive if you want to make your hopes turn into reality and you must be willing to give it your all. What it really takes most of all is energy, the energy to go after what you want and make it happen."

Betty Jensen

"My work is so personally satisfying that I am almost embarrassed at getting paid for what I do."

Dr. Betty Jensen, assistant director of the alcohol recovery unit of a Denver hospital and director of its therapy division, tells you immediately that she is her own most successful rehabilitation story—though her problem had nothing to do with alcohol.

Ten years ago Betty learned that her husband was leaving her after twenty-five years of marriage. "Some people seem to sense these things are coming," she observes, "but it was a complete shock to me. We hear much about the midlife crises of women, but I hadn't the insight then to understand that men, too, go through a frightening period in their forties. I didn't foresee the divorce. I was devastated. I was forty-four years old, I had never worked, and I didn't know where to turn."

Where she did turn was to school. She enrolled at the University of Northern Colorado for a bachelor's degree with a major in psychology. "It was a personal search," she explains. "I wanted to study psychology because I wanted to find out who I was."

Betty chose the school in Greeley, fifty miles from Denver, because her daughter was enrolled there. A second daughter decided to transfer to join her mother and sister, so that two of Betty's four children were now near to lend encouragement and support.

"Of course, it was sometimes a little embarrassing for them," Betty laughs, remembering one professor's shock when he discovered that two of the students in his class were mother and daughter. "You have to realize I really stood out then," she points out. "I was the *only* older student on that campus. It's hard for us to realize just how much things have changed in only a decade. Today there is growing recognition of the needs of mature women. They give college credits for life experience at many schools. Ten years ago I was denied my original college credits because they were more than twenty years old. That was a blow, but some of the anger it generated helped give me the push I needed. I doubled up courses and finished my undergraduate degree in two and a half years. It's only now that I can recognize just how much anger I felt at a society that was so insensitive to my needs.

"My fellow students, however, were very supportive. So many of them told me how much they admired me and wished that their mothers could meet me. That was very helpful."

Going to school again proved a real "high" for Betty. "I was excited to be learning again and to see that I could do it. For years my reading had been limited to seed catalogs. By the time I had my B.S. I was poring over graduate-school catalogs with the enthusiasm of a kid doing Christmas shopping.

"My personal experience determined my direction. I knew that what I wanted was an area of rehabilitation where I could help people to recover and find themselves again after some kind of life crisis."

Betty adds a side note on her career choice that may be meaningful to many women. "Years ago I had taken my original college courses at Purdue in aeronautical engineering. It was during the war and it seemed a promising area for someone with math and science skills. That's still the way I test—strong in math and science. But neither then nor now do I have the slightest interest in those areas. I am interested in people. My work is so personally satisfying that I am almost embarrassed at getting paid for what I do."

Continuing her single-minded course toward career credentials, Betty once again took on a double work load and earned her master's degree in one year. Her actual career focus came out of the field experience that was required of master's candidates. A nearby veterans' hospital was setting up an alcoholic unit and needed help. Betty served her internship assisting in establishing the unit. At the same time the state had passed decriminalization laws on alcohol offenders with provisions for mandatory treatment.

"My experience at the veterans' hospital earned me a job with the Colorado State Department of Health setting up a new drug and alcohol rehabilitation program to comply with the new law.

It was a brand-new area, an exciting, creative challenge. That was the first time that I felt my age as an asset. I looked 'established.' I had credibility. I could generate support from communities. It was a wonderful feeling to know that I was being instrumental in sensitizing communities to the needs of people who required help.

"The only problem was that my job was strictly administrative. I still longed to work directly with patients. I began to think I might do best by opening up a private practice. But that required still more educational credentials. After a time I decided to return to school for the last time, for my Ed.D. My thesis was on "Self-concept," specifically on the impact of the hospital treatment process on a patient's self-esteem. St. Luke's Hospital in Denver was just opening up a new alcohol treatment unit and they allowed me to use it as my research site. They also invited me to return to the staff after I had my doctorate. I am still involved with administration, which I seem to be good at, but as director of therapy I am able now to get involved with patients as well. I truly love my work."

Betty had assumed that her strong career commitment probably precluded any thought of marriage in her future. "I wasn't sure that I had enough energies to do both, for one thing, and it was hard to imagine a man who would put up with me." But a man who respected her goals did appear, and she was happily remarried two years ago.

"My work with alcoholics has taught me a great deal about the dangers of the midlife years. Those women who are able to establish new directions, forge new careers, and restore a sense of purpose in their lives as their children grow up are making the strongest possible investment in their own future mental health and happiness."

Fifty-four-year-old Betty Jensen does not worry too much about midlife crises anymore. She has put her own life back together through a satisfying career and in the process emerged as a stronger, happier person.

5. Going Back to School

For some it means a quick brush-up course in typing and short-hand, for others a commitment of years of study toward an advanced degree. Whatever the goal, the thousands of women who have chosen to return to school—even those who were not particularly interested the first time around—are almost unanimous in reporting benefits infinitely more far-reaching than simply acquiring job credentials. School is often the crucial catalyst in producing a changed self-image, awareness of your own potential, increased confidence, and a set of more ambitious personal goals. Education offers the chance to exercise your mind, expand your horizons, and begin to give priority to some of your own needs and interests.

New schooling is also one of the most obvious ways to prepare yourself for a more meaningful career. So many women have realized this that they have become a major factor on the nation's colleges—have, in fact, revolutionized some of the offerings on campus. Not only are there many new shorter associate degree programs specifically designed to help women qualify for jobs but also there are many more flexible ways to go to school today, schedules that can be blended more easily into the demands of a home and family. A multitude of sources of financial aid are available for women who want to resume their educations after a period of raising children. And recognizing the traumas and uncertainties of returning to the classroom after a long hiatus, schools large and small have devised ways to ease the transition.

It's important to be aware of some of these recent developments because too often a first call to a college for information can be a discouraging experience. Some institutions continue to have rigid schedules and requirements for entrance, but in almost every locality today there are options, good colleges that will welcome you, understand your special problems in juggling school and

79

home responsibilities, and do what they can to make your way a bit easier. There are also new informational sources to lead you to the institutions that best meet your requirements and goals, which you'll learn about at the close of this chapter.

How does it really feel to go back to school at age twenty-five —or thirty-five—or forty-five? For Barbara Artson, now a practicing psychotherapist in San Francisco, enrolling at San Francisco State College at age thirty-three was a turning point. "It was in college that I discovered for the first time in my life that I was actually bright. I never knew that before," she said in a local newspaper interview. "I remember my first day on campus. I was crying. I couldn't believe that after all those years I was finally, officially, in college."

Sharon Nord, who enrolled at Triton Junior College in River Grove, Illinois, after fifteen years at home, talked about the early adjustments in *The Second Flighter,* a campus newsletter directed to adult students: "The first six weeks I was overwhelmed and seriously questioning my choice. It was so hard to study and to adjust. I studied in the kitchen and found that I would keep getting distracted. Every time I looked up and saw a household chore that needed to be done, I would have to get up and do it. I lost a lot of sleep trying to do everything and found myself studying through the late hours of the night, wondering if it would ever ease up. But I learned about better study skills and habits, discipline, readjusting my priorities, and in about the sixth week I could feel a change. Now I look back at that tough transitional time and see my progress and feel so proud of myself. This experience has been great for my self-image. I am learning so much and applying it to my life, taking more risks and not fearing rejection, increasing self-confidence, communicating better with all kinds of people, and understanding people much better."

Like so many women today, Sharon found her return to campus eased by the efforts of her college to help. Triton's program is a prototype of what is available at small schools in many communities. Understanding the many qualms and questions that beset someone who has been away from school for many years, the college offers a free preview seminar where participants can take vocational-interest inventory tests, ask questions about course offerings, and voice their personal concerns to a panel of already-enrolled adults who have volunteered to share their impressions and experiences.

Once enrolled, returnees are offered a variety of minicourses to help them adjust, offering review in areas such as study skills, note-taking, math, reading, and writing. Time organization, memory training, test anxiety, writing class papers, and making class presentations are other topics covered.

Triton has instituted a "Tuesday-Thursday College," condensing courses in a period that allows for easier scheduling of baby sitters and other personal obligations. By attending school two days a week, students can earn an associate degree in three years in majors that include data processing, accounting and business administration, liberal arts, or business management.

The "Week-end College" at Mundelein College in Chicago is another attempt to fit learning into the busy schedules of working adults and mothers with family responsibilities. Mundelein, one of the first to welcome older women, offers career-oriented programs ranging from fifteen courses for a certificate to forty courses for a bachelor's degree. A third of the school's enrollment today is composed of older women.

Colorado College for Women in Denver has devised a curriculum called "Planned Passage," specifically designed to lead to re-engagement in the work force. According to director Judy White, the student and her adviser together devise a personalized course of study, emphasizing sales, finance, accounting, personnel, industrial management, health professions, or medical records technology. Depending on individual needs, women can select a short-term twenty-one-hour program, a thirty-hour course for a certificate, or the thirty-six-hour traditional curriculum leading to a B.A. in management with a major in one of the specific fields offered. A total of 60 percent of Colorado's courses are available at night, and a supervised six-week internship during the course of study gives the opportunity for on-the-job experience.

Shorter certificate programs have been set up to meet the career-oriented needs of returning women in many subject areas.

Fairfield University in Connecticut has a one-year course that includes such majors as communications studies, graphic design, interior design, medical-assistant studies, and paralegal studies. Bentley College in Waltham, Massachusetts, has instituted a six-course program leading to an administrative assistant/supervisory certificate in management, accounting, or data processing with electives in special fields such as pension administration. Mercy College in Westchester County, New York, offers certificate studies in mental health, public safety, private security, health administration, and gerontology. In many cases such programs give beginning qualifications for a job and credits that may be transferred if you elect to go on for more advanced study later on.

It may not even require a full course of study to qualify you for a better job, advises Ann Orul of Chicago's "Flexible Careers." "For example," she says, "many women with 'people skills' feel that personnel or human resources is a likely career choice. The entry-level job in personnel is usually as an interviewer, really a rather routine clerical function. But you can choose selected courses in areas such as benefits, affirmative action, personnel management, or employee relations. Combined with your volunteer-proven ability to work with people you have something far more salable to offer to an employer and a much more promising career path."

Women who can't afford the time required for formal education can find programs today tailored to the needs of working adults and mothers with family responsibilities. "University Without Walls," "Extended Campus," "TV College"—all of these are part of the open-learning concept that has been developed in recent years, ideally suited for adults who missed out on college in their younger days. In many of these programs, learning and your daily life are intertwined, not separate. Programs of study are tailored to your specific interests and goals and you can often earn credits for the knowledge and achievements you have accumulated over the years out of school.

At the College of New Rochelle in Westchester County, New York, for example, women are earning as much as thirty credits —an entire year's worth—for submitting what the college calls a

"Life Experience Portfolio." Contents, according to school officials, have ranged from an account of what can be learned about government from membership in the League of Women Voters to an essay on how a political conservative has evolved into a liberal feminist.

Goddard College in Plainfield, Vermont, is another that will grant credit to students submitting an "Educational Life Experience Petition." Goddard was one of the first to offer nonresident programs for adults who cannot devote the on-campus time required for traditional college attendance. The Goddard Adult Degree Program requires two weeks on campus twice a year to plan with a personal adviser the independent study that the student "contracts" to carry out on her own at home. Many of the projects assumed for credit can be directly tied to a profession. Harriet Gayle, a mother who became interested in nature as a volunteer nature center guide, earned her degree in environmental science from Goddard doing research into many topics she will use directly in teaching on her job. Some twenty-eight other schools, including Antioch, Stephens College, Florida International University, the University of California in Berkeley and in San Diego, the Universities of Massachusetts and Minnesota, and Loretto Heights College in Denver offer similar "University Without Walls" programs.

It's even possible to do your learning without ever leaving your living room. The University of Mid-America covers the four states of Nebraska, Iowa, Kansas, and Missouri via TV. Its courses are broadcast into the homes of four thousand students every day, including many rural residents who have no access to a college campus. Chicago's TV College and New York's Sunrise Semester are long-running TV programs that offer college credits. And there are courses that can be taken for credit via the newspaper, sponsored by the University of California's San Diego extension.

It is estimated that eight out of ten returning students can claim some credit toward a college degree by presenting evidence of past college work or by passing the College Level Examination Program tests, which most institutions use to allow credits for knowledge you've acquired in your everyday living and reading. Subject areas include the humanities, the social sciences, math, and English composition. These tests, administered by the College Entrance Examination Board, are given monthly at testing centers nationwide.

There are also high school equivalency exams open to the 24.6 million women who never completed their formal high-school education. These General Educational Development tests need a minimum of advance preparation since they are designed to measure one's ability to think clearly about ideas and concepts, rather than knowledge of specific facts. Not only will a high school diploma raise your earning prospects dramatically, it also may enable you to think about continuing your education to the level where there is the most dramatic increase in salaries. Across the board, high school graduates earn an average of $5,808 a year; college graduates, $9,162. Contact your local board of education or adult-education department to learn where and when GED tests are given in your area and whether there are courses offered to help you review if you do not feel confident about taking these tests on your own.

Olga Silverstein, a professional family counselor who offers words of advice to re-entering homemakers later in this book, is one example of a woman who received her high school diploma at the age of forty. She went on to college, worked afterward as a social worker in a state hospital, and then received a scholarship and a stipend that enabled her to earn an advanced degree in her field.

For reasons both personal and professional, some women still do prefer to take the traditional route to a B.A. degree. Esther Benjamin, a woman in her forties, enrolled in the full-time program at Northwestern University rather than choosing a more flexible course designed for adults because, "When I decided to go back I was 'snobbish'—I wanted the best school where I could qualify." Esther's original motive was no more complicated than to complete the course she had dropped more than twenty years before to be married. "I always wanted to finish school one day," she says. "Just getting the degree was a goal in itself." But once on campus, she found herself challenged to excel. As a sociology major, she has been involved in a campus study of returning women students and discovered that her high standards were almost universally shared. "Most of these women want 'A's and they are willing to work much harder than their younger classmates to get them. When you taste the excitement of learning once again as an adult, your priorities change. The work is a big drain on your time and energy. But in another way it's energizing to be doing things that are personally exciting and challenging. I consider it the biggest gift I could have given myself."

Major universities, too, have recognized the special needs of adults who are returning, and have devised ways to give them needed moral support. Duke University, in Durham, North Carolina, provides counseling, tutoring, and an innovative program of one-to-one peer counseling to help newcomers with the personal adjustments of their changed life-style.

The University of Maryland also uses peer counselors in its program known as "Second Wind," specially designed for women over age twenty-five. With its own newsletter and information and referral service, tutoring and child-care assistance, and a crisis hotline, "Second Wind" makes every effort to ease the path of its re-entering women. An opening orientation makes them aware of what is available, continuing workshops give help with goal setting, studying, exam-taking skills, time management, and the problems of juggling multiple roles. Maryland offers an "Individual Studies" program that allows returnees with special interests to design their own major in conjunction with advisers.

At the University of Michigan, one of the first centers for continuing education for women, there are refresher courses similar to those at Maryland, along with counseling groups and "brown bag" lunches where returning women can get to know each other. The university has provided enough of its course offerings at night for students who wish to earn more than half the credits needed for graduation in the evening. Special scholarship funds have been set aside for women of promise whose educations were interrupted, and "critical difference" grants are available in case of study-related emergencies. In addition, Michigan has developed administrative management internships for its returning

women students with area businesses, government, and within the
university itself.

The value of on-the-job internships for women is becoming
increasingly recognized. "Continuum" in Newton, Massachusetts, was perhaps the first to come up with a formal course of this
kind in 1975. Continuum's participants work full time at internships four days a week, return on the fifth day for business skills-
building seminars. They work in three different jobs in different
types of settings during their nine-month program, testing out
various career interests. Individual counseling, the setting of objectives, and help with job-hunting techniques are also part of the
curriculum.

"You can literally see the difference in these women from the
time they arrive to the time they leave us," says acting director
Wynne Miller. "One of the toughest problems women face is their
own self-perception. After many years at home they just don't see
themselves as worthy of consideration in the business world. We
believe that a task-oriented challenge, the chance to actually prove
themselves at work, does more for them than any other kind of
education. It not only gives experience and credentials, but also
an understanding of the hierarchies of the working world and
where you may fit in. Any further education has a more definite
focus. By June these women actually carry themselves differently,
walk with a more confident step, have changed the way they dress.
And the shift in their goals from September to June is truly
amazing."

Continuum's alumnae are working in posts as varied as programmer, director of public relations, assistant for pension planning, corporate legal assistant, and marketing specialist. One of
last year's graduates returned to school to study landscape architecture as a result of her interning experience; another enrolled as
a student at the Boston Museum of Fine Arts.

Goucher College near Baltimore began a somewhat similar
program in 1978, but one geared exclusively to management development. It consists of a six-month course giving an overview
of principles and practices of management, followed by a three-
month internship in one of eight major businesses in the city that

have agreed to participate in the program. The intern jobs offered include auditor, insurance sales, sales and marketing engineer, market research analyst, engineering planning technician, research assistant, personnel interviewer, and employee training specialist.

Goucher's program is also attempting to prove the potential of alternative work schedules. Two women share each internship, working half the normal schedule, demonstrating the feasibility and employer benefits of job sharing.

The cost of both these internship projects is comparable to some college tuitions. Other experiments are available on a less intensive —and less expensive—basis. "Project Re-Entry" at Boston's Civic Center and Clearing House begins with vocational testing and counseling; gives weekly two-hour workshops to help assess skills and interests and to build self-esteem and decision-making abilities; and offers its enrollees the chance for a half-time internship in a variety of jobs. The 1979 fee was $750.

Another "Project Re-Entry" began in 1978 at Drake University in Des Moines, Iowa. It also combines workshops, counseling, and personal assessment with a four-month half-time internship, but is unique in two areas. Drake recruits and train "mentors," working women who will assist and advise the interns. And this is one of the few interning projects that operates at no cost to participants. The first demonstration year was funded by a federal grant; the second year was underwritten by participating businesses who pay their interns a stipend to offset the cost of their tuition.

Internships seem extremely successful in their goal of reintroducing women to the realities of the working world and letting them see some of their own potential. If the idea appeals to you, check to see whether such programs are available in your community. If not, you might want to approach a business with an internship proposition on your own. Be wary, however, that you do not allow yourself to become an unpaid clerical worker. Internships are intended as educational, skills-building experiences, and any employer who becomes involved is obligated to provide job training beyond the kind of entry-level positions you could be performing for pay.

Another type of career education you might want to investigate
are the trade and technical schools in your area. Though trade
schools sometimes have a poor reputation because of a few un-
scrupulous operators, the good ones offer training in job-oriented
skills that qualify you in a relatively short time for jobs in specific
areas, from airline personnel and advertising art to brick masonry
or blueprint reading. Labor-union and government-sponsored apprenticeship programs for "blue-collar jobs" are also beginning to
open up to women. Many of these can be more rewarding finan-
cially and otherwise than the more common women's occupations, according to Muriel Lederer, author of a book called
Blue-Collar Jobs for Women.

Mrs. Lederer interviewed a number of women working in these
nontraditional fields and reports that they find many advantages
in their occupations. "An aircraft mechanic, for example, earns
nine dollars to ten dollars per hour. And more importantly for
many of these women, their job ends promptly when the shift ends
—there's no 'one more letter' that must go out after five o'clock.
That's important for women who have family responsibilities,"
she points out.

"Women who have taken jobs repairing business machines
sometimes receive paid company training, earn a salary around
three hundred dollars per week, plus a travel allowance, and
receive a company car. And they are not tied to a desk all day.
They have freedom and independence. Women working at this
kind of job—as well as repairing TV sets, watches, washing machines, automobiles, and many other similar mechanically oriented occupations—are often pleased at the daily opportunity to
show their competence and solve problems for other people.

"It isn't always easy to be a pioneer, however. There can be
negative feelings from male coworkers who are not used to having
women around. It takes a mature attitude to be able to handle
these situations. But it seems that women who have taken the
trouble to get specialized training are not easily frightened away.
It takes effort and commitment, but they are truly pleased to be
where they are."

Mrs. Lederer believes that many women simply don't come to

grips with the number of years they will be in the work force. "They settle for low-paying jobs," she says, "thinking they will be temporary, then find themselves stuck there." She strongly recommends considering the long-term prospects before "settling" for just any job. Learning trade skills can be a worthwhile investment in upgrading your working potential.

With so many schools offering so many kinds of varying programs, it is almost impossible for an individual to keep up with all of the new opportunities as they become available. In recognition of the growing need for a central source of educational information and counseling, the National Center for Educational Brokering has been established in Washington, D.C., with the goal of setting up branches across the nation. The job of the educational broker is to match the potential student with the most suitable educational opportunities for his or her particular needs and goals.

Congress has supported this movement with Title IV of the Educational Amendment of 1976, calling on every state to establish educational information services, and most have done so. States such as Kansas and Delaware now have a toll-free telephone referral service. Almost all states have at least a referral office in their education departments. Meanwhile, hundreds of colleges and private agencies have become involved in disseminating information. One of the first and largest of these, the Regional Learning Center of Central New York in Syracuse, estimates that in its first four years it provided information referrals and workshops for ten thousand upstate New Yorkers and individual counseling for fifteen hundred others. The University of Wisconsin Extension's community-based educational counseling for adults now operates in forty of the state's seventy-two counties and has already served more than four thousand clients. In New Orleans, WYES, the public television station, has become involved through a series of monthly live sixty-minute TV shows providing information for women as potential students. It visits the various locations where postsecondary education is available, deals with the financial implications of returning to school, with the feelings of insecurity and inadequacy, and with the family adjustments that face women who want to return to school. A directory of educational and career-information services for adults is available for $2.00 from the National Center for Educational Brokering, 1211 Connecticut Avenue NW, Suite 400, Washington, D.C. 20036.

Education is expensive, but there are many sources of financial aid for women who want to go back to school. Some institutions, like the Universities of Michigan and Minnesota, have special scholarship funds set aside for this purpose. Regional aids are available from all kinds of sponsors. Philip Morris, Inc., for example, offers funds for women over twenty-five in its home cities of Milwaukee and Louisville. The Diuguid Fellowships are designated for Southern women over age twenty-one.

Aid is available to all women over thirty through the Loving Care Scholarship Program sponsored by Clairol, Inc., which allots $50,000 annually for this purpose. Since it began in 1974, this project has helped more than four hundred women to complete their educations on full- and part-time bases. Recipients have ranged from a beauty-salon owner in Texas to an alcohol treatment center co-ordinator in Florida to a university instructor in Minnesota, the latter having returned to school after twenty years of homemaking.

One of these scholarships enabled Houstonite Pamela Rafferty, a mother of three, to attend school full time after her divorce instead of working at part-time jobs while she pursued her studies. Mrs. Rafferty, a two-time Clairol winner, advises all women to research carefully into all of the available funding sources. "No one had even told me about the Clairol program," she says. "It was just chance that I happened to see an announcement on a bulletin board."

Other national scholarships are available through the Business and Professional Women's Foundation and the Soroptimist Clubs. There are also grants for study in specific fields and numerous government loans and grants to be investigated.

If you qualify as a "displaced homemaker," someone with no recent work experience who has become responsible for her own support after a number of years at home, you can get information on many newly available training programs, educational opportunities, and scholarships by writing to Displaced Homemakers,

Business and Professional Women's Foundation, 2012 Massachusetts Avenue NW, Washington, D.C. 20036.

See the Appendix for other sources of information on financial aid.

Earning a college degree is important to many women as a sign of self-worth and as an important addition to a résumé. But there is one caveat attached to returning to school. If you are using this path as an escape from the traumas of job-hunting, be aware that you are only postponing the inevitable. And don't expect your degree to excuse you from the necessary transition of a beginning-level job if you have no work experience.

Helen Kaplan, who earned a Master of Business Administration degree from the University of Connecticut at the age of thirty-seven, hoping to gain access to higher pay and a more interesting job, is one of many who found the realities of the business world different from what she expected. "It took me a year and a half to find a decent job," she relates. "I had no business experience, yet was considered too old for the usual beginner jobs. No one would hire me. I had to settle for doing market research for $3.50 an hour for a while. Finally, at a dinner party, I happened to meet someone from a local company who listened sympathetically to my tales of job-hunting. Weeks later, when there was an opening at his company, he remembered me and called me. I was hired as a marketing assistant, the bottom rung. The other person at that job is twenty-five years old and has no M.B.A., just a couple of years of retailing experience."

Though her degree gave her added knowledge and the potential for moving up, it did not eliminate Helen's difficulty in finding a job nor spare her a necessary period of learning on the job. Nor is it realistic to expect that you will automatically solve your re-entry problems because of schooling.

There are many women who still believe that the best kind of preparation for moving up remains the oldest path—as a secretary. Helen Stuart, who began her advertising career through this route, says, "Getting in is the most important thing. It remains true from what I see that in the so-called glamour fields like advertising, the easiest entrée is as a secretary."

Constance Scanley, who rose from secretary to manager of community affairs in a seven-year period at Pitney-Bowes, concurs. "I always advise women to get in the door any way they can. Don't take just any secretarial job, of course," she cautions. "Get into the department where you want to move ahead. Then take on responsibility, look for chances to learn and grow, make yourself visible. You'll likely be recognized. Most companies prefer to promote from within."

Adds Gloria Lanza, one of the speakers at the Tishman Seminars, "I looked upon my two years as a secretary as a kind of on-the-job M.B.A. It was my education in business."

Education, then, can come in many forms. The real purpose of learning is to stretch ourselves, to become all that we are capable of being. Sometimes we do that best just by getting out and testing ourselves. Often a career direction and a corresponding educational path are clearer after some actual work experience. "You can't always see where you might fit best until you're actually working in the field," believes Helen Stuart.

So by all means consider schooling—but consider carefully. And consider the possibility of working first to clarify your future goals, particularly where advanced degrees are concerned.

If you decide you want to go back to school, you're in good company. Some thirty million adults—one out of every five—are currently enrolled in some form of education or job training to make their careers more meaningful and rewarding. If you choose to join their ranks, there are more kinds of opportunities than ever before, more flexible programs, more ways to help finance your goals, and more ready resources for finding out what options are available to you.

All that is needed further is your own commitment.

Carolyn Di Mambro

"Interning gives you the chance to get out there and prove what you can do."

"It was the first time in my life I had had the luxury of looking around and deciding what I wanted to do. But how was I to start? You can't just go knocking on a company's door and say, 'I think I might be good at something here.' "

At age thirty-six, Carolyn Di Mambro has found something she is good at and something she enjoys immensely. As director of Masspool, Inc., a van-pooling plan for commuters funded by the Massachusetts Department of Transportation, she serves as broker between a van-leasing company and employers, setting up commuting pools for employees in areas where there is no public transportation. It is a job that requires salesmanship, planning, co-ordination, and knowledge of the public transportation system. "I love it because it is full of variety, demanding of my skills in many areas—some skills I knew I had and a lot of others I had better come up with in a hurry," Carolyn says, obviously enthused about the challenge.

Transportation is a field that has always interested Carolyn, but something she feels she might never have gotten into on her own. Her entrée was Project Re-Entry, a work internship program sponsored by the Boston Civic Center and Clearing House.

Carolyn was married in 1963, earned a B.A. in history and English at the University of Iowa one month before her first child was born in 1964, and had her second child in 1967. "My husband was in dental school, so I worked when I could to keep us going. It was always part-time office work, on and off, with no pattern or ongoing plan—just for the extra money. Finally, when my husband was settled in his practice, we bought a house and I thought at last I could afford to stay at home. Well, I kept busy for about a year fixing up the house, and then I found myself woefully underemployed. But here I was, thirty-four years old and with no idea of what I really wanted to do. I read about Project

93

Re-Entry, an internship program for on-the-job training, while looking for volunteer work in the *Boston Globe*. Interning seemed a chance to prove to myself as well as to other people that I could do something more than I had done in the past.

"There were about sixty choices of internships. I chose the Massachusetts Bay Transportation Authority. The job was in marketing and promotion, an area that seemed to offer opportunities. Most of all, here was a field that I had always been drawn to, an opportunity to learn something.

"The internship was supposed to last for six months, but a few weeks after I started, my supervisor left his job. It looked like disaster, but it proved to be a real opportunity, one that lasted a year and a half. They were short-staffed, so they gave me responsibility simply because no one else was available. The Transportation Authority was about to reproduce schedule cards and timetables for various transit routes. I researched a new kind of bar graph to show the routes, the points of interest along the way, the approximate time between stops. To do this, I rode the routes, talked to the drivers and to the stationmasters in the garages. I learned how the unions operate, and a great deal about the whole system.

"The internship was half time. I needed to work full time to get the job done, and I said that was fine if I got paid. So I became a paid consultant, starting at $4.50 an hour. The real disappointment came when they turned my job into a regular position—and I had to train my own replacement, because it is company policy to promote from within. You can't take the internship as a sure ticket to a job where you work.

"Fortunately, a new project came up and I was hired again to divide my time creating route maps and other informational aids for the Customer Service Section and supervising the new Pass Program Office. My consulting fee was increased to $8.00 an hour. Meanwhile, there was a local election, a change in administration, new people in charge at the Transportation Authority—and I was out of a job again.

"At about that time one of the managers in my department suggested I apply for the position of director of the newly created third-party van-pool program called Masspool, Inc. He knew they were looking for a director for the new project but had not been satisfied with the applicants so far because none had transportation experience. He told me I might have a chance at it because of my experience. I got the job—and I love it."

Working full time has proved no major adjustment for Carolyn. In fact, she has found it better than part time in terms of eliciting help from her family. "With a part-time job, no one at home seems to realize why you can't do all that you did before. Now I get a lot of help at home. My husband has been very supportive and, in fact, initially encouraged me to plunge into the internship experience.

"Because of his willingness to help, both physically and emotionally, I have been free to pursue a career I might otherwise have had to forsake. In this house, all four people clean and wash dishes. Two of us shop while the other two wash and iron. The kids cook every weekday night. I'm very proud, in fact, to come home and find four or five kids standing around watching my kids cook. Their friends can't believe it.

"The children have learned to be very independent. At twelve and fifteen they take the commuter train to their dentist and doctor appointments. They ride their bikes to swimming lessons, and take responsibility for many of their own decisions. There's no reason why I must stay at home. *They* don't!

"I believe that the interning experience was beneficial to everyone in the group. At the start, I was so proud of what I was doing I wanted to tell everyone about it. Then I stopped talking because so many people asked me why I was dumb enough to want to pay for the privilege of working. I can only say that the experience to me was the equivalent of a master's degree. Why should you feel you have to go back to school when interning gives you the chance to get out there and prove what you can do?"

Gladys Gifford

"I just needed more . . . I wanted to get my mind cranked up and moving again."

Happily ensconced in a roomy, charming old Victorian home in Cambridge, Massachusetts, Gladys Gifford had a life many would have envied: successful husband, sound marriage, four healthy children, summers on Nantucket, and enough serious volunteer interests to keep her more than occupied, interests that ranged from conservation to politics to concern for the future development of her community.

What motivates a woman like this to subject herself to the sacrifices and rigors that go with entering law school at age thirty-seven?

"I just needed more," says Gladys, a soft-spoken, intense woman of obvious intelligence. "I got tired of working for no pay when the people I was working with were paid, particularly on my last major volunteer project, a new land-use plan for Cambridge to save the town from overdevelopment. But I had no credentials, no training. I was neither a planner, an architect, nor a lawyer.

"I had thought about going to work earlier," she recalls, "but in much more traditional terms. I love to cook and I considered a food-related business. I even took a few part-time jobs to learn about the field. But they bored me. And I felt that if I made cooking my vocation, I would lose it as a pleasure.

"So I talked to people, searching for a career that would be satisfying over the long haul. The important thing was that I wanted to get my mind cranked up and moving again.

"I had married right out of college and watched my husband go through the agonies of law school. I barely saw him for three years. It was hardly a tempting prospect, but given my interests and activities over the past fifteen years at home, it was the option that seemed to make the most sense."

The first obstacle in her path was the law board exam, a frightening thought after so many years away from school. "I was

96

terrified, especially of the math. I bought all the preparation manuals in print, all the sample tests, holed up in the library, and hardly came out for two months while I tried to refresh myself on math problems and grammar rules that I had long forgotten," she remembers.

With the test out of the way and acceptance at Boston's Northeastern University Law School in her hand, Gladys set out to restructure her family life to allow the time she would need for studying. "I realize I am very fortunate," she says, "because I was able to bring in a wonderful and loving part-time housekeeper. Without that, I don't know if it would have been possible.

"Then, my husband was terribly supportive. Since he is established in his field and his hours were more flexible than mine during this period, he took over things like dental appointments and attending school plays and helping the children with their homework. And the kids have done their bit, too. They took over their own social lives. No more was I available as family planner and chauffeur, so they became responsible for making their own plans and getting places on their own. And with all that help, I still had to become superorganized at home to make sure that things ran smoothly."

With graduation almost in sight, Gladys can look back on the grind with humor. But she does not minimize the work required, especially the first year at law school. "It was books, books, books all the time, all week, nights, and weekends. Often I'd doubt if it was all worth it. I was so panicked when I had to take exams I had to get counseling to overcome my anxieties."

Yet she was enjoying it. "It is a school that is very supportive to women, and one with a number of students in their thirties, forties, even their fifties. And I liked being back in school, liked the kids and the informality, liked having a separate world of my own where no one could reach me. What a luxury to have totally uninterrupted time in the library, time to ponder a problem and work through to the solution with no other demands on me."

Her study has paid off with a job offer even before her graduation. Northeastern University operates on a work-study program that alternates three months of study with three months of practi-

cal work experience. On one of her work stints, Gladys was asked
to return as assistant district attorney for Middlesex County, Massachusetts, a job she will begin just as she turns forty-one.

The job excites her. "It's a chance to be a trial lawyer almost
full time," she explains, "a skill I want to learn, and a field that
currently has few women. I want to learn to be an advocate. The
field will be wide open for me if I'm good."

She does, however, recognize the negatives to the change in her
life. "I had to drop many things I cared about deeply, causes I had
worked for for years. And I became cut off from many old friends.
They somehow didn't seem as comfortable with me anymore. And
then I had so little time. I learned to doubly value those friends
who understood and took the initiative in keeping in touch.

"I have no more free time," she reflects. "And I have to be
careful. There is sometimes tension if I try to ask too much from
my husband. He is with me, but he can't jeopardize his own work
because of my needs.

"Finally, there is the guilt. It can't be avoided. I wish I had
more time to spend with the children. I feel particularly bad for
my daughter, the youngest. I have one more free summer before
I go to work. I don't know how I'm going to face it after that when
I have to tell the children we can't go to Nantucket for the summer
anymore. I recognize the ambivalence in these thoughts, and I
have found to my surprise that they are shared by many women-
mothers of my generation. I am torn between my biological reality
as a mother and my emotional and intellectual needs.

"But I have to keep my future in mind. My sons are sixteen,
fourteen, and twelve. The oldest is already off to boarding school,
the next goes this fall, and after that, before we know it, they'll
all be peeling off. And of course it's nice to be able to supply some
extra income for all those school tuitions ahead."

A trade-off. An exciting and challenging new career that leaves
too little time for other elements in her life. Weighing the alternatives, Gladys Gifford has decided that the sacrifices are worth the
promise.

6. Putting Yourself on Paper: The Résumé and the Cover Letter

You're on the way. You've learned as much as you can about yourself, analyzed your skills and interests. You've learned enough about the fields that appeal to you to make an educated choice of directions. You've looked into the ways you might add educational credentials to better your chances in the job market. There's just one step left before you are ready to begin your job hunt: your résumé.

A résumé is important as a last exercise beyond its function as a job-hunting tool. Putting it together should provide a review and a wrap-up of all you've learned about your own abilities and goals. As a concise summary of your assets documented by your past accomplishments, it should serve as a framework for selling yourself in person as well as on paper.

Be clear as you begin as to what a résumé should be—and should *not* be. You are not writing your life story. You can and should be selective, choosing to include the things that reflect most favorably on you, omitting what might work against you. If your volunteer background is fragmented, you'll want to pick out only the parts that work toward your career goal. And you need only put down the information about you that is relevant to a job. You don't have to announce your marital status, your age, or the ages of your children, you shouldn't try to list your hobbies or pet charities or where you were born—unless you feel that these facts are somehow related and helpful to your work objectives.

What you do hope to achieve is a sketch of yourself and your work capabilities, one that will make you come alive as a unique person with enough promise so that an employer will want to meet you in person. You are actually writing an advertisement for yourself, and like all good ads, you'll want to concentrate on your strongest selling points.

It's going to take several drafts to get the résumé right. For starters, it helps to do a preliminary inventory sheet, using the work sheets from the earlier exercises you've done to help you. Here are the things to include on your inventory:

1 WORK HISTORY. List all of the jobs you've ever held, full time, part time, free-lance, or volunteer. For each, give the name and address of your employer, give yourself a job title, detail your duties, and note the dates you were employed.

2 SKILLS CHART. List the skills you uncovered as your strongest work assets. Put down specific examples of instances where these skills were used successfully in the past.

3 EDUCATION. List the schools you attended, the degrees you received, any special courses you have taken aside from formal schooling, and any academic honors or awards you have received.

4 CAREER GOALS. Name the kinds of work you hope to be doing five or ten years from today, then list the jobs you could be seeking right now to prepare for these goals, as in the sample inventory below.

JOB INVENTORY
Elaine Brown
6616 Hastings Avenue
Columbus, Ohio 43215
(614) 682-8743

WORK HISTORY

1 *Camp counselor*
Camp Owego, Arlington, Ohio
Summers, 1958, '59, '60

Supervised 12 youngsters
Taught swimming and canoeing skills
Organized and directed camp dramatic shows

2 *Secretary*
Rogers Advertising Agency
Cleveland, Ohio, 1961–64

Researched competitive advertising in various product categories
Co-ordinated projects and acted as client liaison
Originated new client reporting form for agency account executives
Handled correspondence and travel arrangements

3 *Fund-raising and publicity aide*
Columbus Congregational Church, 1964–71
Publicized special events through posters and newspaper and radio
  announcements
Assisted with various fund-raising projects
Helped plan and man sales project bringing in $25,000, a 30 percent
  increase over any previous fund-raising endeavor

4 *Children's program co-ordinator*
Columbus Museum, 1971–74

Organized three seasons of free weekend programs for children
Researched and recruited speakers and performers for programs
Supervised all arrangements
Co-ordinated publicity

5 *Room mother (teacher's aide)*
Howard Elementary School
Columbus, Ohio, 1973–75

Co-ordinated parent participation in school activities
Recruited volunteers
Chaperoned class trips

6 *Library aide*
Howard Elementary School
Columbus, Ohio, 1973–76

Assisted with all phases of library operation
Guided children in book selections

7 *Membership administrator*
Firehouse Co-operative Nursery School
Columbus, Ohio 1974–76

Screened prospective applicants
Compiled school information packet
Investigated alternate school enrollment procedures
Improved recruiting and admissions systems, upping enrollment by
    10 percent

8   *Voter-information Director*
   League of Women Voters
   Columbus, Ohio, 1976–78

   Researched background of district political candidates
   Interviewed candidates for views on current issues
   Wrote public-information brochure summarizing candidate
      qualifications and opinions
   Supervised citywide distribution of voter-information brochure
   Expanded circulation to an additional 20,000 suburban residents
   Recruited volunteer manpower and co-ordinated schedules of
      voter-information telephone service

SKILLS USED IN VARIOUS JOBS

Writing
2. Prepared research reports
3. Wrote news releases
7. Compiled school information packet
8. Composed voter-information brochure

Research and Analysis
2. Analyzed competitive advertising campaigns
4. Researched potential speakers and entertainers for special events
7. Investigated alternate school enrollment procedures
8. Researched and interviewed candidates

Administration
1. Directed dramatic shows
2. Co-ordinated schedules
2. Improved client reporting system
4. Managed series
4. Co-ordinated publicity
5. Recruited and scheduled volunteers
7. Improved recruiting and admissions procedures
8. Supervised telephone service
8. Supervised distribution of brochures

EDUCATION

B.A., Ohio State University, 1961; English major, education minor
Adult education courses in sewing, modern art
Introduction to business management course, Columbus Community
    College, 1979

CAREER GOALS

1 Director of public information
    Starting jobs: Information assistant
                Secretary to information director
2 Director of research
    Starting jobs: Research assistant
                Administrative assistant in research department

Now you must select from and arrange this material in the way
that gives you the most credentials for the jobs you want most.
You'll want to have one master résumé that is always available for
use, but if you have more than one job target, you may find it
helpful to have more than one résumé. The strongest résumé is one
that is pegged toward a particular job, and the skills and experience you want to emphasize may vary considerably from one
position to another.

Generally, résumés are organized in one of two ways; by the
jobs you've actually held, or by the functions or job skills you have
demonstrated successfully. You should do a draft each way to see
which works better for your particular background.

The first format, a chronological record of your experience, is
easier to prepare, quicker to read, and more familiar to employers.
But it is not always most advantageous for a returning homemaker since it tends to point up employment gaps. You may be
able to get around this by some judicious use of your volunteer
experience, but it will require careful effort to make this kind of
résumé effectively use a diverse set of past accomplishments to
relate to a specific future goal.

The functional résumé, on the other hand, concentrates on
marketable skills and avoids time references. The one drawback
here is that some employers are suspicious of this approach pre-

cisely because it avoids mention of concrete work history. Some people remedy this by including a very brief job history at the end.

Whichever format you use, it is absolutely imperative that your résumé, the picture you are sending out to represent you, looks its very best. See that it is professionally typed, use high-grade paper, and have it reproduced by offset, not by mimeograph or Xerox machines. The layout should be attractive and easily legible, with wide margins and plenty of white space. While it is preferable to condense into one page, it is better to use a second page than to make the first one crowded and hard to read.

Make every effort, however, to keep your résumé as concise as possible. It is estimated that an average employer spends five seconds scanning a résumé. Your top selling points need to come out loud and clear—and in a hurry. Break up the information into categories so that a reader can find what he wants to know quickly. Don't use unnecessary words or long sentences. Instead of "I was responsible for," say "managed"; instead of "I was involved with planning, organization, and counseling," say "planned, organized, and counseled." Use active verbs, single space between sentences, double space between paragraphs, and try using bullets to highlight information.

Here's a suggested outline for your first résumé draft:

1 PERSONAL DATA. Begin with your name, address, and telephone number. Any other personal data are optional and belong at the end.

2 EMPLOYMENT OBJECTIVE. If you are definite about the kind of job you are seeking, state it here. If you have more than one objective, you may prefer to omit this on your résumé and include it in a cover letter instead.

3 WORK HISTORY. Choose the form that presents your qualifications most favorably:

a. Start with your most recent employment and work backward. For each job list dates of employment, name and address of the employer, the nature of the business, and the position you held. Describe your job in terms of regular duties, special assignments, scope of your responsibility, and number of people you supervised. Highlight your specific accomplishments, using concrete facts and figures wherever possible.

b. List the functions you have performed capably in the past, selecting those most related to your present job objectives. Describe specific examples.

4 EDUCATION. If this is one of your strong selling points, list it before your work history. Include the names of schools you have attended, degrees or certificates received, and (if you wish) dates of graduation. Omit high school if you have a higher degree. Put down major and minor subjects and any specialized courses that are relevant to your work goals. Include honors or any special recognition you received.

5 MISCELLANEOUS. Give any special information that may pertain to your field of work, such as knowledge of a foreign language, pertinent volunteer activities or hobbies, ability to operate special equipment, membership in professional organizations, articles published, awards or honors received. (Remember, *only* include work-related information.)

6 REFERENCES. You may give the names and addresses of three people who have direct knowledge of your competence or may simply state, "References available on request." Be sure you have obtained permission of the persons you use as references.

As you work out your first drafts, be sure that your job titles and descriptions of your work duties and skills are couched in professional terms. Instead of "chairman," call yourself a "manager," "administrator," or "co-ordinator." Instead of committee member or volunteer, put yourself down as "administrative aide" or "assistant." If you served as president of an organization or as a top officer, it is not exaggeration to call yourself a "chief executive" or "executive officer." And your activities as a high-level volunteer were probably not so different from those of a business executive, a point to make clear to others by once again adapting business jargon to describe them. For example, here's a possible summary of the work of almost any president of a PTA or church auxiliary:

Directed 100-member organization

Headed 10-member executive board

Set agendas and chaired meetings

Represented organization on city and statewide councils

Initiated 12-month plan to expand operations, improve worker participation

Supervised projects that expanded annual income by 10 percent

Sheila Lummis, whose interview appears later in the book, is an example of a woman who managed to put her volunteer leadership roles into special perspective by finding a pattern, one that she called "creating educational change in society." Perhaps your own activities also have a pattern of direction that can be expanded upon in your résumé to make them more meaningful.

Using our sample inventory sheet as a starting point, here are further samples of how a woman with two possible job goals—a position as an information specialist or as a researcher—changes her emphasis and format to make her case stronger in each direction.

Elaine Brown
6616 Hastings Avenue
Columbus, Ohio 43215
(614) 682-8743

JOB OBJECTIVE: Public-information assistant

WORK HISTORY

1976–78 *Director of voter information*
        League of Women Voters, Columbus
Researched background information and personally interviewed
        district political candidates
Wrote information brochures comparing candidate qualifications and
        views on issues
Supervised citywide distribution of brochures expanding circulation
        to an additional 20,000 suburban residents
Managed telephone information service for voters

1974–76 *Membership information administrator*
        Firehouse Co-operative Nursery School, Columbus
Compiled and distributed school information packets for prospective
        enrollees
Held informational interviews and evaluated applicants
Introduced new information and recruiting techniques that led to a
        10 percent enrollment increase

1971–74 *Children's program co-ordinator and publicist*
        Columbus Museum
Organized and publicized three seasons of free weekend programs for
        children

Researched and recruited speakers and performers
Supervised all program arrangements

1964–71 *Publicity aide*
  Congregational Church, Columbus
Responsible for publicizing special events through posters and press
  releases for newspaper, radio, and TV

1961–64 *Administrative assistant*
  Rogers Advertising Agency, Cleveland
Wrote competitive advertising reports
Co-ordinated projects and acted as client liaison
Composed correspondence and interoffice reports

EDUCATION: B.A., Ohio State University; English major

REFERENCES: Available on request

Elaine Brown
6616 Hastings Avenue
Columbus, Ohio 43215
(614) 682-8743

JOB OBJECTIVES: Research, administration

EDUCATION: B.A., Ohio State University; English major
  Management training courses, Columbus Community
  College

SPECIAL SKILLS

RESEARCH AND ANALYSIS

Researched and compared competitive advertising campaigns
Compiled policy positions of district political candidates through
  research and personal interviews
Investigated alternative membership recruiting techniques
Prepared resource list of potential speakers and entertainers for
  special-events series
Analyzed and improved upon client reporting procedures

WRITING

Prepared research reports
Wrote press releases

Composed voter-information brochures
Compiled membership-information packets

ADMINISTRATION

Co-ordinated citywide distribution of voter information
Set up and supervised telephone information service
Revamped school recruiting procedures, increasing enrollment by 10
    percent
Planned and managed special-events series
Instrumental in sales project that upped annual profit by 30 percent

WORK HISTORY

1976–78 Director of Voter Information
            League of Women Voters, Columbus
1974–76 Membership administrator
            Firehouse Co-operative Nursery School, Columbus
1971–74 Children's Program Co-ordinator
            Columbus Museum
1964–71 Administrative aide
            Columbus Congregational Church
1961–64 Administrative assistant
            Rogers Advertising Agency, Cleveland

REFERENCES: Available on request

As you can see, these résumés have culled through both paid
and volunteer experience to pick out accomplishments that work
together to create a strong picture of ability in particular areas.
They do not attempt to include every volunteer job, and they
arrange dates so as to eliminate obvious gaps in working, using
Elaine Brown's continuing participation in her church to cover the
years when she was mainly at home caring for small children. The
fact that she has been a homemaker since 1964 has not kept her
from making a strong case for proven skills that are readily transferable to the business world. When Elaine arrives for an interview, she has given herself a head start in demonstrating that she
has potential as an employee. And she has given herself a framework for discussing her work strengths in person, since she has
edited her variety of volunteer experience to give a definite focus
toward a particular kind of job.

Work to accomplish this same kind of focus for your own résumé. Keep refining, looking for stronger verbs to describe your work and accomplishments, and pare down your language wherever you can. When you are confident that you have done the best you can, you'll find it extremely helpful to ask outsiders to critique your draft even further, particularly anyone you know who sees résumés frequently as part of his or her job. Here are some of the things you'll want to know from your friendly critic:

1 Is the résumé attractive and easy to read? Does it look professional?
2 Is it easy to get a quick picture of your work qualifications?
3 Have you given strong enough information to document your abilities?
4 Is there any unnecessary or extraneous material?
5 Will it make an employer want to meet you?

Having worked so hard to perfect this résumé, you may be somewhat chagrined now to be told that you may not always want to use it to get yourself an interview. But there are circumstances where you might be better off emphasizing just one part of your background or using the strength of a strong personal reference to gain access to the person you want to see. In those cases, a letter may be all you need by way of introduction. Here are two such instances.

Mr. Harold Collins
Director, Department on Aging
State of Arkansas
Little Rock, AR 72205

Dear Mr. Collins:
Joanne Davis, director of the Indianapolis Senior Center, tells me that the state is about to undertake a survey of the nutritional needs of older adults. As a founder and current president of the Indianapolis Meals on Wheels service, I have particular knowledge in this area that I believe would be extremely helpful to you in this undertaking. I have, in fact, initiated this very kind of research on a somewhat less formal basis in Indianapolis, managing a volunteer staff of fifteen. I feel certain that I could be valuable in co-ordinating your survey efforts in this area as well

as in other parts of the state.

I would like very much to meet with you to learn more about your staffing needs for this project. I'll phone you early next week in the hopes of setting up an appointment.

Thank you for your consideration.

Sincerely,

Carolyn Gray

Though her complete résumé may indicate additional skills that might be of interest to some employers, in this case it is Carolyn Gray's particular knowledge of the nutritional needs of the elderly that gives her an edge for the job, and throwing in unrelated experience might actually weaken her case against competitors.

Mr. Alan Roberts
President
Roberts Business Machine Company
1745 Las Bresas Boulevard
San Diego, CA 92111

Dear Mr. Roberts:

George Davis, president of the Davis Manufacturing Company, has told me that you have an opening for a research assistant in your sales department. He suggested that I contact you, as he felt that my background and abilities might be of interest to you. I will be in touch this week by telephone in the hope that we can meet to discuss this further.

I will look forward to talking with you.

Yours truly,

Ann Watkins

Again, a résumé might have been included with this note, but the writer chose not to send one because she has just completed work for her degree in marketing, has no work experience, and felt that her strongest recommendation for a job was the reference referred to in the letter. She is playing her strongest card, hoping that once she is able to get in for an interview she will be able to sell herself better in person than on paper.

Writing a cover letter is an art in itself, even when it is accompanied by a résumé, because a well-written letter allows you to call attention quickly to your top selling points, whether they are work skills, special knowledge, or an important reference. Every letter you send should be individually addressed to a specific person with a proper title, never to "Personnel Director" or "To Whom It May Concern." If you have knowledge about the particular organization you are addressing, you can word your letter in a way to make it known that you have taken the trouble to do a bit of research. A cover letter normally should be short, never more than three or four paragraphs, and should close with a request for an interview. Conciseness and smooth writing are important; remember that this letter is a sample of your communications skills. Needless to say, the typing should be neat and without errors in spelling or punctuation.

Here are a few examples of effective cover letters:

Mr. Arthur White
Public Relations Director
Whitney's Department Store
Portland, OR 97211

Dear Mr. White:

Recently I learned from Dr. Ann Logan at the University of Oregon Journalism School that you have an opening for a community-relations assistant in your department.

My many community contacts through leadership roles in organizations such as the local Women's Club, Symphony Orchestra, Library, and Community Chest should prove valuable in introducing the store's recently inaugurated noontime special-events series to a wider audience, and I have a number of ideas for additions to this series that I would like to discuss with you.

I can show you samples of successful publicity releases that I have written for many of these organizations. I've recently broadened my skills by completing my degree from the University of Oregon with a journalism major.

For your review, I am enclosing a résumé of my background. I'll be in touch in the hope of setting up an interview so that you can consider my work and how I may be able to make a contribution to your department.

Sincerely,
Pauline Harris

Dr. Marlene Darrow, Co-ordinator
Career Counseling Services
St. Paul Extension, University of Minnesota
St. Paul, MN 55823

Dear Dr. Darrow:

My experience in counseling students regarding career and educational choices may be of interest to you as you set up the new St. Paul counseling office for the University of Minnesota.

The enclosed résumé will indicate the range of ages and backgrounds with which I have worked, and my success in helping to establish a similar program at the YWCA.

I believe my past work would make me valuable to your office, and I would like to arrange an appointment to discuss how my abilities might best meet your needs.

Thank you for your consideration. I'll phone for an appointment and will look forward to meeting you.

Sincerely,
Ann Carter

Mrs. Agnes Moore
Personnel Department
The Warren Company
11 Arbor Street
Wilmington, DE 19806

Dear Mrs. Moore:

Thank you for your time on the telephone yesterday.

I was most impressed to learn about the diverse activities of your department. After we spoke, I looked up the report you had mentioned and I feel even more certain that my skills at interviewing and devising training programs would fit well into your expanded efforts in this area.

My résumé is attached to give you an idea of the scope of my experience. I'd like to make an appointment to discuss this further with you. Would Wednesday, March 11, be convenient for you?

I'll be in touch hoping to set a definite time. I look forward to meeting you.

Sincerely,
Shirley Brown

While everyone agrees that a letter should quickly arouse the reader's attention and interest, there is some argument as to whether you should try to be clever, using a "gimmicky" or trick approach. Some employers see this as showing ingenuity, while others may be turned off. If you have an original idea that is businesslike and in good taste, you may want to experiment with it. Carol Blair, whose interview follows, found a "gimmick" was just what she needed to attract attention and gain entrée to employers.

Gimmick or not, all good letters have one thing in common: They emphasize reasons why an employer should want to meet this particular applicant. It's an approach you'll want to take one step farther when you move on to the next part of your job search, the interview.

Carol Blair

"The person I was recommending was me."

Carol Blair credits a letter of recommendation with getting her the job interview that led to her rapid rise to manager of personnel at Sherwin-Williams Company in Cleveland—a letter she wrote for herself.

"I was angry," she says. "I had gone back to college for three years, worked hard, and earned almost a straight A average. But when I answered an employment-agency ad for a management-training program, I was told that the only kind of job I was likely to get in business was as a secretary. I had been a secretary fifteen years earlier, with only one year of college to my credit."

Carol sat down with her husband, a sales and marketing executive, to figure out a way to "market" her own potential to business. "What we came up with was gimmicky," she admits, "but it worked. I wrote a letter of recommendation for a person qualified for management—someone with business experience and college training in English—someone who would do well in customer service or public relations or personnel. I closed the letter saying that the person I was recommending was me. That letter got me a number of interviews and two jobs offers, one with a bank management program and another in the Sherwin-Williams personnel department.

"I chose the second job," she explains, "even though the starting salary was less than I could make as a secretary, because I saw opportunity for growth. The department head had planned to be there only temporarily and she seemed to view me as capable of being trained to take over. Incidentally," Carol adds as an aside to job hunters, "one of the reasons she had been impressed by my letter was that I had taken the trouble to find out her name rather than just addressing my letter to an anonymous 'Personnel Director.' It had taken a day of research to come up with all the proper names to write to, but it was well worth it.

"When I started working, it took only a few months to realize that I was changing as a person," Carol says. "I realized that I was very ambitious, that I wanted to move up. I worked hard, put in long hours at the office, got up early in the morning to work at home. In addition, I was working for a manager—a woman—who gave me every opportunity and helped me to grow rapidly. I went back to school at night for my master's degree in business administration, this time at the company's expense. In my first nine months on the job, I devised a new performance-evaluation system for nonexempt employees. Within fifteen months I had been made manager of the department, and in four years' time I had more than tripled my income."

It was a major transition for a mother of three who had quit college after a year and worked only occasionally after her marriage, always as a secretary and only to help out a bit when family finances needed a boost.

"But I always knew that I wanted to finish my education, and as soon as the children were all in school, I felt it was my time to begin."

Carol was thirty when she enrolled at a local community college, a venture she describes as "culture shock" when she found that her fellow students were mostly seventeen or eighteen years old. "There were half a dozen of us who were older—returning veterans and a couple of women. We gravitated together for moral support." Her teachers, she found, were very supportive and encouraging—at least until she graduated with an English major and was considering continuing for an advanced degree. "They told me not to bother, that there were no teaching jobs and Ph.D.s were finding themselves out of work. So I determined that I would try to find an interesting job in business. If that didn't work out, I would consider going to law school in another year when I had saved some money. What happened was that I went from being immersed in literature and poetry to becoming fascinated by business. It was exciting and challenging to me."

The change in Carol took some serious adjustments at home. "It was difficult for my husband," she reflects honestly. "There were two particularly hard times. When I went back to school and was doing so well, he was proud, but he had mixed feelings. But the ultimate effect turned out to be positive because it motivated him to go back to writing, an interest he had put aside for years.

"The next period of strain came when I went to work and went back to graduate school in the same year. I was preoccupied and it was a tough time. But as I moved up, my income grew. Now my husband tells me he is waiting for me to do well enough so that he can afford to stay at home and write.

"He made sacrifices for me. He was unhappy in his job and wanted to take another position on the East Coast. But we waited a full year to move until I had enough management experience behind me to find a good job."

With the help of another carefully thought out letter, outlining her rapid professional growth, Carol was able to generate interviews in her new home in New York State and to find an excellent position as manager of personnel at Savin Business Machines Corporation.

As a personnel director who now sees many re-entry women looking for work, Carol strongly advises women to do their homework in advance and come in with a definite job goal in mind. "To say, 'I'll do anything with a chance for growth' won't work, even if that is the way you feel," she says. "There are few general jobs available. We work with specific openings. You have to have definite job objectives, even if you are not sure they will ultimately prove the right ones." One area she recommends as a good entry-level position for mature women is customer service, where verbal skills and problem-solving abilities are assets.

"I found my maturity an advantage when I returned to work," she states. "It meant I could better relate to managers on their own level. I know much better today how to get things accomplished than I would have when I was younger. It has enabled me to move up faster.

"What I did not foresee was the change my career would make in our life-style. We seldom entertain anymore, tend to want to spend time together rather than going out with a group. And I found that many of my old friends were uncomfortable with the 'new' me. They just didn't understand why I wanted to do this with my life."

Why did she do it? "It is exciting," she repeats, "a challenge. When I took this job I was thirty-nine years old and I told them I intended to become an officer in a major corporation. I meant it."

You leave Carol Blair feeling sure that she will achieve her goal.

7. Getting in the Door

Your résumé is ready. You've polished up your letter-writing skills. Now, where do you go with them?

If you've been thinking about working for a while, chances are you've been reading the want ads. You've seen the jobs that are advertised and the names of the employment agencies whose business it is to find jobs for people. It might seem that this is the obvious approach to finding your own job. You answer the most promising ads, visit the employment agencies with your résumé. And for good measure, you get a list of local businesses and send out a batch of résumés to their personnel directors.

That's just the way most people do go about looking for work. And if you're lucky, you might get a job this way, too. But the odds are against you.

What Color Is Your Parachute? made the best-seller list by pointing out that these traditional job-hunting techniques don't work well for people who want more than a job just like their last one. As someone who has been out of the work force for a while, it's definitely not the best route for you, either.

Here's why. Want ads usually garner dozens of replies, and you're likely to run up against a lot of people who seem to offer more than you do in terms of relevant experience for the job—at least on paper. Very often when this happens, you won't even get the courtesy of a reply to your letter. One reason companies use anonymous box numbers is to save themselves the trouble of having to send out polite rejections.

Employment agencies are geared to fill particular job openings, and they, too, operate on the theory that similar experience is the prime requisite for a job. Though you may find an exception, it's the rare employment counselor who will take the time to sell your promise to a prospective employer if there are other candidates on hand with more obvious qualifications.

Sad to say, most personnel departments work the same way. They have specific openings to be filled, most of them with job descriptions specifying a certain number of years of similar experience. They aren't paid to take chances on people.

None of this is to say that you don't have a chance at a job this way. But you're definitely doing things the hard way and leaving yourself open to a lot of discouragement.

Another reason to seek a different approach is that most good jobs never are advertised and don't even filter down to the personnel department. The number of jobs that are handed outside of a particular department to be filled comprise only about one third of the total number of job openings. The better jobs are filled internally or through word of mouth—and many a new position comes about only because someone convinced an executive that there was good reason to create it.

You have a lot to offer to an employer, more in terms of maturity and life experience than many of the people who are competing with you. You've discovered how many work skills you've acquired while you've been constructively "unemployed." And you've found a direction where you have good reason to feel you will succeed. Now you need to find a way to get in to see the people who will recognize your potential and have the authority to hire you. You need to mount a campaign, not by passively answering ads or applying to agencies, but by compiling a list of targets and actively going after them.

You're going to need two target lists. On the first one goes everyone you know or have known who may have knowledge or contacts in the field you are aiming for. That means friends, relatives, friends of friends, neighbors, doctors, dentists, accountants, lawyers, people you've served with on committees, people you've met at parties, people you knew in college, ex-employers, ex-teachers, even ex-husbands—anyone you can think of who may know someone who will know of opportunities in your field. Personal contacts are the key to getting in to see the level of people you need to meet. And it's often the only way.

So you can't be bashful about asking for help. You are *not* asking any of these people to hire you. You are asking for their advice and guidance, and most of all, for the names of other people you may approach for additional counsel and information, using your original contact as a reference.

Once you begin seeing people in positions of authority, the odds begin to work in your favor. If you are persistent and your network continues to grow, somewhere along the way someone will know someone who needs and wants what you have to offer.

You should include the names of the people you talked with earlier when you were researching various career possibilities. Tell them you've decided to make their field your choice and ask for further advice on names of people to see. Each call, each interview should increase your list of contacts. Always stress that you are not asking for a job, but for leads, counsel, and information. Most people will be willing to help you on that basis.

Your college alumni office may be helpful here. As was mentioned earlier, some have lists of working alumni who will act as resource people for returning homemakers. More and more schools are making their job listings available to older alumni as well as to new graduates. Get in touch and see if they can help you. Ask for a copy of the latest *College Placement Manual,* a listing of the positions customarily offered to college graduates by principal employers. The back of this free book gives both occupational and geographic listings of hundreds of companies and may suggest some leads in your own locality.

That's the beginning of your second list, the organizations that are your potential employers. To fill this list you must do some careful combing of business directories. Here are some standard sources of information available in most libraries:

STANDARD INDUSTRIAL CLASSIFICATION MANUAL *(SIC MANUAL).*
Classifies and assigns numerical code to industries and lists both manufacturing and nonmanufacturing concerns by titles, alphabetically and numerically, by their SIC numbers.

STATE INDUSTRIAL DIRECTORIES. List nearly every company that does business within each state and give considerable information about the products, sales, officers, etc. Companies are listed alphabetically, by town and county, and by products and services. Each company has an SIC—Standard Industrial Classification—number, which clearly defines what the company manufactures. The SIC number consists of four digits, such as

2811. The first two are the major group number (28), the third digit is the subgroup number (281), and the fourth digit is the specific industry number (2811).

DUN AND BRADSTREET *(D & B)*. Gives company names, addresses, phone numbers, annual sales, total employees, SIC numbers, names and functions of divisions, and executive names. Also listed geographically, by SIC numbers and by product classifications.

STANDARD AND POOR'S REGISTER OF CORPORATIONS, DIRECTORS, AND EXECUTIVES. Register of directors and executives includes names, business, home address, school attended, graduation year, and positions held. Corporations directory lists companies by SIC numbers and alphabetically, and contains a geographical index.

KLEIN'S DIRECTORY OF DIRECTORS. Directory of corporation directors and executives.

MOODY'S INDUSTRIAL MANUAL. Comprehensive source of information on industrial corporations, with capital structure tables, financial statements, and statistical records of selected companies.

Other reference directories:

THOMAS REGISTER OF AMERICAN MANUFACTURERS
DIRECTORY OF CORPORATE AFFILIATIONS
COLLEGE PLACEMENT ANNUAL

Local and state manufacturers registers
Directories for local chambers of commerce, trade associations, and foundations
Special industry references for areas such as accounting firms, consultants, executive-search firms, advertising agencies, insurance companies, securities dealers, research laboratories, banks, educational institutions, etc. And don't forget the Yellow Pages!
Newspaper business and financial pages, helpful for names of people who've been recently hired or promoted as well as news of interesting new projects in local organizations.
Business publications such as *Fortune, Business Week,* and *The Wall Street Journal;* same as above but on a national level.

Other publications that may provide useful information are *Ad Search,* a compilation of executive, technical, and management ads from sixty-eight Sunday papers, *MBA, Working Woman, Vocational Quarterly Journal, College Placement Council Salary Survey, and Collegiate Woman's Career Magazine.* Most good-size libraries carry these periodicals, which are further sources of business news about specific companies and executives.

For each company you list, you'll want to note names of specific people to be approached, those who are in a supervisory position in the areas where you hope to work. If you can get to these people through a personal contact, you're way ahead of the game. You're going to use list No. 1 to help you reach the names on list No. 2.

But if all else fails, try a direct approach. Write a strong letter and be persistent (though pleasant) about following up by phone. You can't sell yourself unless you get in the door. You must find a way to get yourself inside. Here are a couple of notes that may give you some ideas for approaching strangers.

Mr. Garfield Wyatt
President
Albuquerque City Bank
1 Main Street
Albuquerque, NM 87102

Dear Mr. Wyatt:
    Since your bank is the leading financial institution in the city, I'm sure you are already aware of the growing numbers of women who are managing their own finances today and could benefit from professional guidance in this area.
    From my wide community contacts as a long-time active resident of Albuquerque and as a recent widow who had to learn firsthand how to handle my own financial affairs, I feel uniquely qualified to expand the bank's efforts in helping other women with these matters. I have several specific ideas for bank-sponsored seminars for women that I have outlined and would like to share with you.
    I hope you will agree that this is a neglected area with much potential for performing a public service while attracting new customers for the bank. My résumé is enclosed for your further information. I'll be phoning for an appointment and look forward to discussing this further with you.

                                            Sincerely,
                                            Sally White

Mr. Elliot Conway
Marketing Director
Little Industries
16 Water Street
Houston, TX 77002

Dear Mr. Conway:

As a newcomer to the marketing field, I have been researching local companies and am particularly impressed with the accomplishments of Little Industries in this area.

Since you head this division, I hoped you might be able to find a few minutes to talk with me, offering advice and guidance on the best career path to qualify me for this kind of work and the opportunities for employment in Houston.

I'll be most grateful for any information you can give me, and will be in touch by phone to make an appointment.

Thank you in advance for your help.

Sincerely,
Joanne Murray

When a personal contact is involved, the note becomes simpler:

Mr. Alden Perry
Marketing Manager
General Products Company
111 Alden Avenue
Tampa, FL 32932

Dear Mr. Perry:

George Gaines, sales manager of the Acme Company, suggested that I contact you.

I am a recent college graduate interested in the marketing field, and Mr. Gaines indicated that you were an ideal person to offer knowledgeable advice and guidance on the opportunities in this area.

If you can find a few minutes to talk with me, I'll be most grateful. I will phone your office to make an appointment.

Thank you in advance for your help.

Sincerely,
Patricia Lane

If you have special knowledge of a particular field through your early education or your later interests, you'll want to scan the directories carefully for companies where your expertise may give you a competitive edge. Patricia Boer of Indianapolis, after thirteen years at home, found that her college biology major helped her gain a job as a sales analyst with a company that sells diagnostic equipment to hospitals. She had begun by researching the companies in her city that had any connection with biology, a total of three. Her present employer, the one located closest to her home, was the first place she visited.

"Even after all these years, my educational background made the equipment terminology more meaningful to me than to the average person," she explains. "Combined with some basic ability with math, the company saw that as sufficient qualification for a job analyzing the computer runs that come in from the salesmen in the field. It's my job to translate those figures into information that is meaningful to the company. Once they saw potential, they were willing to teach me the mechanics of my job on the job."

Katherine Cranley, former wife of a doctor, discovered that her personal knowledge of the health-care field gave her entrée to a job with the new Health Maintenance Organization in Baltimore. "I knew the health field was where I wanted to be. When I tried hospitals, all I was offered were typing jobs. So I looked into sales opportunities in the field. I believe that is the easiest way to get in the door and the quickest way to prove yourself," she says. Her assignment was to explain the new health-care plan to prospective customers, businesses in the area. "Selling is tough, but you have great visibility and measurable results. It's also a way to spot other opportunities. I'd say I was offered a job a month while I was out selling."

With some experience under her belt, Katherine enrolled at night for a master's degree in business administration, a move that told her employers she meant business about her career. She was moved to her present position as assistant to the executive director, where she is being trained for an executive position of her own.

Both these women found that what started as an exploratory meeting turned into a job interview. While you can't and should not count on this, it does happen and it's well to be prepared, just in case.

In any event, there's no question that you will eventually be having interviews for specific job openings and it's time to talk about techniques for selling yourself and handling your interviews with ease.

Sheila Lummis

"I made it through pull and persistence. And the key thing was contacts."

Vibrant, auburn-haired Sheila Lummis looks every bit the successful businesswoman she is today: senior corporate underwriter for one of the nation's top public television stations, former manager for community affairs for a *Fortune* 500 corporation.

Six years ago, at age thirty-seven, this mother of five was out looking for her first paying job. A dissolving marriage was, as she puts it with a wry smile, "making it clear that I was going to have the opportunity to prove that I could support my children."

Sheila's work qualifications consisted of an outstanding record as a volunteer and a commitment to community betterment. "You name it," she says, "I did it. I was active in my college alumni association, the local Republican Women's Club, the PTA, the community chest, local health services. But in order for that to add up to anything, I knew I had to evaluate what I had done, to find a pattern that would be meaningful in a résumé. Some careful analysis of my activities began to suggest that pattern. Everything had been aimed in some way at creating educational change in society—and always from a position of leadership. The organizations I chose were those with the potential to create change. And I had felt that I would only be effective in them if I became a leader.

"For example, I felt the sex education in our school system was terrible. To do anything about that as a parent, I had to become involved in the PTA. And if I hoped to accomplish my goals within the group, I had to do more than join—I had to become the *president* of the PTA."

Sheila used books to help her translate her volunteer work into a professional résumé. "But books that were intended for men," she states, "books that used the terms and language men in business were accustomed to hearing." *Executive Search Unlimited* by Carl Bolles is one she recommends highly.

"With no working experience to list, my résumé was slanted in terms of results. I never used the word 'volunteer.' I talked about accomplishments, and wherever feasible, I put in figures, especially those that reflected growth. I had two job objectives—public relations and community affairs—and I used my experience to document my ability in those two areas."

Getting a job was far from easy, she found. "I made it," she reflects today, "through pull and persistence. And the key thing was contacts. I approached the men in corporate life whom I had known socially or through volunteer activities, those who knew my abilities, and asked if I could use their names to ask for interviews.

"After I had succeeded in my job, many women came to see me for advice. I always suggest this route. We all know people who could be helpful. But so many women are reluctant to use their valuable contacts. It has something to do with our conditioning. We freely give favors, but hate to ask them. Women need to realize that this is how the system works. And people who allow you to use their names do this because they feel you will reflect well on them. When they send in a competent person, it is a credit to *them*."

Sheila's job targets were narrowed by the fact that she wanted to work near her suburban home and preferably for a large corporation, one that would quickly establish her professional credentials.

"I knew that my chances were best in a company that had a philosophy in sync with my own, one that was interested in social change in society. I did a lot of homework, read dozens of annual reports, and zeroed in on about a dozen possibilities. But the more I learned the more I knew that the one place I really wanted to work was Xerox.

"So I wrote directly to the chief operating officer of the company—and in the first line of the letter, I used the name of a contact who was equally high in the corporate world. It's imperative to see a decision maker," she advises, "someone at top-level management. For a woman without work experience, personnel departments are simply a dead end."

In response to her letter, Sheila got an appointment with the chairman's assistant. It seemed a very promising interview when they met in October, but in December Sheila was told there was no room for her in the new budget. She did not give up.

"I tried another route, writing to the head of the communications department, which encompassed public relations and advertising. I made a fatal mistake in that interview," she recalls with a laugh. "I told the man I thought I could be helpful to him by relieving him of many of the details of his job. It turned out that he was a man who loved attending to details. The last thing he wanted to do was to give them up. I hadn't done a very good job of finding out about the man I was going to see!"

Still determined, Sheila would not give up. She went to an outside consultant who worked with Xerox. "He was a thinker who had input into the company's directions and access to the chairman," she says. "It was this consultant who went back to the first man I had seen months before and told him he felt I would be good for the department.

"I felt reasonably confident at that point, so I had a big tag sale, and used the proceeds to treat myself to a much-needed vacation. When I got home, I called (they never called me back, incidentally —I had to do all the calling, always), and at last the answer was 'Yes.'

"At this point I made another mistake," she says. "I had done my homework in making my choice of where to work and in seeing the right people to get the job—but had not done my homework in terms of salary. I had not found out the salary range for the kind of job/position I had been seeking. And like many women, I was so relieved to be offered a job, I didn't try to negotiate after I knew they wanted me. I began at a salary that was too low and forever after I was handicapped because of that starting level."

Sheila's first job was as a program administrator for the Xerox Fund, a post that required making recommendations on which projects were worth corporate support. Next she became program director, designing and developing a structure for Xerox employees to contribute to their communities with company support.

Her innovative program let employees choose up to three projects yearly to fill unmet needs in the community, working as a group on their own time but with the corporation rewarding their efforts with up to three thousand dollars per year to support each project. The advantages of her plan were many, with employee relations and company loyalty high among them. It was the only program of its scope in the country, and the guidelines, structure, and training for the project were all Sheila's doing, aided by the knowledge of volunteerism she had gained as a stay-at-home mother.

From that post she was promoted to manager of the company's community affairs, combining corporate contributions with other activities of the company, such as promoting art exhibits in four major markets, a program that combined philanthropy with some very sound customer relations. By the company's standards, Sheila was an enormous success.

But she had problems. Though she had more than doubled her salary in four years, she had reached a plateau and could not see herself advancing farther where she was. She felt it was time to move on. "I didn't really want to leave," she sighs. "I had a dream job, even though I was probably trying to do too much. But it was necessary for me to make more money. Women can't settle for traditional job progress pace if they start late. Time goes by so quickly. We have to get in there and get our credentials as professionals, spend enough time to learn each job, then move on."

Her only chance for more money at Xerox would have been to make a career shift within the company. She was offered a job in field sales, with the expectation of becoming a branch manager in two years. "At that time there was only one woman with that job out of ninety-six managers, and it is lucrative," she says. But it means working sixteen hours a day. I knew my personal limitations as a single mother. You have to decide whether you can afford to pay that kind of price.

"I had thought at that point of becoming a consultant to other corporations because I had developed expertise at something others could use. It would have been easier for them to deal with me as a consultant, since they wouldn't have had to worry about where to put me in the corporate structure. But once again, knowing myself, I knew that my own business would turn into a seven-day-a-week thing. Again, it didn't seem the right thing at this time."

Meanwhile, as she was weighing her options, Sheila was busy putting together Xerox underwriting and promotion of a public television special on the life of artist Georgia O'Keeffe. Following that, New York's educational Channel 13 came to her with an offer to become their senior corporate underwriter, to set up similar underwriting with other corporations. The salary was more than a third higher than she was making.

"I took the opportunity," she says, "for a new kind of learning experience and a salary this time appropriate to the work involved."

This is not likely to be Sheila's final career move. Her family is growing up. With only three of her five children now at home, the demands have lessened enough to allow for the commuting into New York City that her new job entails. She has attained the credentials she wanted so badly at the start—and they are credentials that leave the future wide open for a talented woman who has forged a successful career out of her own personal dedication to a better society.

8. Putting Your Best Foot Forward: The Interview

Job interview: two words that can cause the most confident to develop a severe case of nerves. We've already mentioned that job hunters have symptoms so similar they have been given names like "interview insomnia." And no wonder, for now you are laying yourself on the line, asking for a particular position, and risking rejection.

Just a word about that fear of rejection before you go any further. There's no real reason to be afraid, because you *are* going to be rejected during your job search—and it is no reflection on you or your abilities. No one is offered every job they apply for. You won't even want every job. Sometimes your personality and that of the interviewer simply will not gibe. That's nobody's fault. Sometimes the position will simply be wrong for your qualifications and skills. And there will be instances when another person is just plain better qualified for this particular job.

You must be prepared to expect a certain number of rejections and still know that eventually you are going to succeed. It's just a matter of having enough interviews to get to the right job. And since you can't know ahead of time when that special job is going to appear, you approach each and every interview as though it is precisely the job you want—because it may be, or it may lead to that job eventually. Even the unsuccessful interviews are helpful as trial runs, chances to polish your ability to present yourself effectively. The résumé was your advertisement; the interview is your showcase, the place where you merchandise your talents. You want to approach each one prepared to convince the interviewer that you have something important to contribute to his or her organization. And practice does make perfect.

Always come prepared with knowledge about the company or

organization you are visiting. You should know its products or services, standing in the community, the number and kinds of jobs that are available. Ask people you know in the business community, and if possible, talk to people who have worked there. You can learn a lot also by getting a copy of the annual report, the company newsletter or magazine, and any other information they may have available to the public. When you can, an excellent way to get this information is by visiting the building. You may sense a great deal just from the atmosphere and from talking to the receptionist. And you'll be able to double-check driving directions or bus routes, where to park your car, and how much time to allow for travel. Always, always allow extra time for travel. Arrive early for the interview. Nothing is more likely to destroy your composure than arriving late and flustered.

Remember that first impressions can be crucial. Don't underestimate the importance of appearance. If you have been talking about losing that extra five pounds, now is the time to do it. Neatness definitely does count. See that your nails are just right, your stockings just so. Invest in the best haircut you can afford and a smart conservative suit with a becoming blouse, something that makes you look like the successful businesswoman you aim to become. Choose an outfit that you feel comfortable in, not one with collars or bows that may need constant adjusting. Nothing does more for your morale than feeling confident about the way you look, and when you feel good it shows in your walk and your overall mien.

That kind of body language is important. You want to give an image of poise. Shake hands firmly and look the interviewer in the eye. Sit up in your chair and be alert. Don't fidget.

Since many of the questions you'll be asked in job interviews are predictable, you can rehearse ahead of time and be ready with good answers.

You'll almost surely be asked to "Tell me about yourself." Have clearly in mind a brief review of your background with emphasis on why it leads to your present career goals. Be able to relate just what you have to offer and why it should be of interest to this company, something you've learned by doing your homework on the organization's current directions and needs.

Here are some other very common interview questions that you can study ahead of time:

What brings you here today?
Why are you interested in this field? This company?
How would you describe yourself?
What do you consider your chief strengths on the job?
   Weaknesses?
Which of your past jobs have you liked best? Least? Why?
Can you tell me what's important to you in a job?
What were your last supervisor's strengths? Weaknesses?
Would you tell me about your best supervisor?
What are your job objectives for five years from now?
What makes you believe you'll be qualified for that position?
Where do you see yourself going in this company?
What kind of people do you work with best? What kind of people
   do you find most difficult to work with? How do you handle
   this kind of person?

While you want to come off as friendly and outgoing, you also want to remain businesslike when you answer questions such as these. Don't ramble. Let the interviewer control the interview. Your answers should be complete, but brief and concise. State your qualifications with confidence, but not with exaggeration. Know what you have to offer and know your ultimate goals. If you have sent or brought your résumé, use it as a guide in presenting concrete examples of your accomplishments and skills. If the interviewer mentions that the job will entail areas you have not listed on the résumé, try to supply additional instances from your past that might give you relevant qualifications.

Be prepared to be asked to elaborate on some of your statements with comments such as "Can you explain that a bit?" or "Could you tell me a little more about that?" That's par for the course, a way to draw you out. When you're asked a complicated question, it may help to give the answer in list form, giving you time to think and organize your answer. For example, if asked about your strengths, you might say, "First, I think I'm a well-organized and efficient person; second, I get along well with people; and third, I have the capacity to stay with a job until it is completed."

Then you can give examples to back up your statements.

Some interviewers like to throw in broader questions such as "Where do you see this industry going?" or "What are the broad issues that you think a company like ours should be attuned to in the next five years?" This is a way of testing out your frame of reference and your intellectual curiosity.

All of these questions and others like them have a definite purpose. The interviewer is trying to judge certain things about you. These include your ability to think logically and express your ideas clearly, to grasp the meaning of questions, and to organize your replies. You're going to be sized up as to your ability to get along with people, your attitudes, your maturity, character, and sense of values, your future potential as a supervisor.

Different interviewers have different styles of accomplishing these objectives. Some like to leave things loose and see where you will take the conversation. Others have a rapid-fire style of questioning that will force you to think quickly and answer concisely. You may run across a few people who want to see how you will respond to a hostile question. Others like to see what happens if they allow the interview to lapse into silence. A good defense against this last ploy is to have questions ready about the job or the company. The more interviews you have, the more you'll begin to sense certain patterns and learn to handle them.

Though it's illegal, you may very well be asked about your age, the ages of your children, what provisions you've made for their care, and even whether you belong to any women's liberation groups. You don't have to reply, but if you really want the job, you just might be better off giving direct, unemotional information. (You can always reform the place *after* you get hired.) And, of course, you'll have a ready reply when you are asked why you want to go to work in the first place.

Knowing what to expect, you can not only outline what you want to say to these and other likely interview questions, but also you can and should rehearse your answers out loud. Ask your family or a friend to do some role-playing with you, giving yourself a chance to refine your interview techniques. If you own a tape recorder, listen to yourself. You may hear things you never expected in your tone of voice or your choice of words. Listen carefully to your vocabulary, your grammar, and your punctuation. They matter.

Even more important than what you say is how you say it, how you project yourself. When all's said and done, most jobs are won on the basis of personal chemistry between the interviewer and the applicant. Your warmth and charm, your energy and enthusiasm and optimism will say more about you than any other kind of job qualifications. Approach the interviewer just the way you would approach any new acquaintance you hope to turn into a friend— with good will, openness, and candor. Let the interviewer get to know you, the best side of you.

Under no circumstances should you be apologetic about the years you've been away from the work force. They've given you a wider perspective, a knowledge of human nature, the ability to get along with people, a sense of responsibility. You've had the opportunity to organize and supervise and counsel and pursue myriad interests that might not have been possible within the confines of a nine-to-five job. If you know this and truly believe it, you should be able to convince your prospective employer that your maturity is a tremendous advantage.

While you're anxious to please this interviewer, remember that you are doing your own interviewing here. This is your chance to appraise the job, the employer, and the firm, to decide if the job meets your career needs and whether this is the kind of place you want to work. Don't hesitate to ask questions about the company and the opportunities for advancement. Be sure that you have a definite understanding about the nature of the duties of the job you are discussing.

It's well to keep a written file of your interviews, rating yourself after each one. Here are some of the questions to ask yourself:

How did the interview go overall?
What points did I make that seemed to interest the employer?
Did I present my qualifications well? Did I overlook any that are pertinent to the job?
Did I miss opportunities to better sell myself?
Did I learn all I need to know about the job?

Did I forget or hesitate to ask about factors that are important to me?
Did I talk too much? Too little?
Was I tense?
Was I too aggressive? Too timid?
Based on this experience, how can I improve my next interview?

Here are some of the negative factors that lead to rejection of job applicants as reported by 153 companies surveyed by Frank S. Endicott, director of placement at Northwestern University:

Late to interview without good reason
Poor personal appearance
Overbearing or aggressive
Inability to express oneself clearly
Lack of planning for career—no goal
Lack of interest or enthusiasm—passive, indifferent
Lack of confidence and poise, visibly ill at ease
Lack of tact
Lack of courtesy, poor manners
Condemnation of past employers
Lack of vitality
Failure to look interviewer in the eye
Lack of knowledge of field of specialization
No knowledge of company
Cynical
Intolerant

A few additional interview tips directed specifically to the re-entering women in Hunter's Tishman Seminars by two seasoned interviewers are these:

"Don't come on too strong at the beginning," suggests Lloyd H. Dalzell, vice president for executive development, R. H. Macy & Company. "Let the interviewer take the lead. Don't make statements about yourself unless you can back them up with something specific and positive. Remember that you're more likely to create excitement in an interviewer through your own enthusiasm. No matter how many times you've been turned down, remember that nobody has ever gotten every job they've applied for. You have to be 'up' for every interview."

Thelma Straw, employment relations analyst, J. C. Penney

Company, notes, "Your attitude is the major thing in an interview. Strong commitment and having a goal go a long way. You have to be clear about your strengths and objectives and your own self-esteem. We simply don't have the time to do career counseling. You should come in able to say, 'I'm interested in working for your company because _____. I feel I could do _____ for you because I am _____. And your résumé should indicate your strengths clearly."

Somewhere along the way the interviewer is going to ask you to name the salary you want. Be prepared. Find out ahead of time what the pay scales are for comparable work. Most applicants try to get around this question by asking what the company's range is for this job, but a canny interviewer will evade your question and ask you to give him a figure. Don't undervalue yourself because you think it's the only way you'll get a job. You can always agree to a counteroffer if your asking price is too high. But once an employer is interested you may well get what you ask for, so long as it is within a realistic range for the job. It's certainly worth a try at getting top dollar for your labors.

As you must have gathered by now, looking for a job is a full-time job in itself. It takes research, patience, and endless persistence. Perhaps it will help to remember that almost everyone goes through this some time in their lives. You can feel virtually certain that if you see enough people, pursue enough leads, and keep your belief in yourself, you will indeed get a job. Just don't be discouraged if it doesn't happen overnight. Three or four months are minimum for most people; six to nine months of looking are not uncommon.

In cases where the interview seemed to go well but there was no immediate opening, you'll want to make a note to call back in a month or two to see if there has been any change in the hiring situation. It can't hurt to let the employer know that you are still available and interested. Lots of applicants have come by since you applied, and even if he or she liked you, it's entirely possible that you've been forgotten. A reminder may be all it takes to put you back high on the list.

After every interview, good or bad, a thank-you note is in order.

It's more than politeness; it's an opportunity to summarize once more your qualifications for the job. Here's a sample follow-up letter:

Dear Mr. _____:

Since our meeting of January 18, I have given a great deal of thought to the prospects of a career with the Martin Company, and I want you to know that I remain extremely interested in the position we discussed.

I was impressed with the caliber of your company and its strong commitment to continued leadership in its field. I believe that my own background of working successfully to obtain co-operation and enthusiasm from all levels of personnel would contribute to the continued effectiveness of your employee-relations department, and I am enthused about many of the ideas we discussed to make this part of the company even more active. I hope very much to have the opportunity to join your staff and help achieve these exciting goals.

Thank you for your time and consideration. I look forward to hearing from you.

Yours truly,

_____

No one will deny that job interviews can be traumatic. But they are also exciting—a chance to meet interesting people, learn about a lot of interesting organizations, an opportunity to learn how to present yourself with poise and skill. Look at your interviews this way, as learning experiences. Keep your sense of humor and your perspective. Whatever may have gone wrong today, tomorrow may finally bring the right interview for the right job.

If you go into each interview confident about what you have to offer, if you've done your advance preparation and know what kind of job you want and why you want to work for the firm where you are applying, sooner or later things are going to click. You're going to get that first job.

But before that happens you should have begun making changes at home, changes to help make your transition to the working world as painless as possible for everyone.

Margaret Klee Lichtenberg

"The important thing is that each of us has been able to help the other achieve what we really wanted."

There was never a question about Margaret Klee Lichtenberg's potential as a writer. Winner of prizes all the way through school, by the time she graduated from the University of Michigan she had received four Avery Hopwood writing awards, won the *Mademoiselle* magazine college fiction-writing contest, and was awarded a Woodrow Wilson Fellowship to Harvard.

But Margaret had other ideas. She was in love. Her husband-to-be was also a talented writer—and a very traditional male. He had difficulty accepting this kind of competition from the girl he wanted to marry. "It was 1963," Margaret says. "I was twenty-one years old. I wanted to get married. I had no support at home for personal career ambitions. No woman in my family had worked after she was married. My fiancé wanted a traditional wife. So we made a silent pact. I would give up my writing if we got married. It's only now, sixteen years later, that we can look back and recognize where we were at then."

The young couple used Margaret's prize money to travel in Europe for five months, then settled in Rome, where Margaret learned the language and became a proficient Italian cook while her husband worked as an interpreter in a local press office. "I had a baby boy and lived the life of a typical middle-class Italian woman," Margaret recalls. "I had physical symptoms to tell me something was wrong, but I ignored them. Often I would get up in the middle of the night to write poetry secretly."

Margaret and Jim Lichtenberg continued to lead a conventional life when they returned to New York three years later. Jim took a job writing advertising and publicity copy—not the kind of writing he wanted to do, but a good job suitable for a man supporting a growing family—for Margaret was now pregnant with her second child.

"It was the birth of that child, my daughter, that changed me," she states with conviction. "It was like being reborn myself at age twenty-eight, like being Alice in Wonderland going down the rabbit hole and coming out completely transformed. The natural childbirth experience itself was extraordinary. I was elated. I wrote a seven-page poem about the experience. I became aware for the first time of what it meant to be a whole person rather than playing a role. Being a writer was part of me and I would no longer deny it. Curiously, it was the childbirth experience that gave me the courage to look at our life together in a new way and to communicate my troubled feelings to Jim.

"The atmosphere at home had been tense because neither of us were happy with what we were doing. Yet each of us had been afraid to risk talking about it. Jim hated his job. He wanted to write—and so did I. When we finally confronted how unhappy we each were, we decided to start fresh. Jim quit his job. We put our furniture in storage. We took our savings and returned for three months to Europe, where we both really began to write. Our marriage changed. For the first time my husband began to share in caring for the children. When we came home we tried a different kind of life, moving to a cabin in the woods north of San Francisco. It was a fruitful period for us creatively. Both of us were beginning to sell our work. But we found that the rural life-style was not for us, that we missed the stimulation of the city.

"It was when we came back to New York that reality hit us—and our marriage was in real trouble. We had no money and two young children. We couldn't afford two free-lance writers in the family. The tensions became unbearable. We even separated briefly. But neither of us really wanted to end the relationship, and Jim went out and got a full-time job again as a gesture of how much he wanted the marriage.

"One thing the separation had accomplished was to make it clear that we couldn't blame each other for what was wrong, that we had to look into ourselves for our own compromises and solutions. Once we saw that, everything else worked out eventually. It was a struggle—sometimes it still is—but in the years that followed we've managed to alternate periods of working to help each other to seek out the career satisfaction we need.

"I wanted out of the house by then. My youngest child was in school a full day. I was ready to get out into the world. I hoped to find a job in publishing. But even with published writings of my own, I was thirty-two years old and had no work experience. The job search was arduous. I wrote to every publishing company, starting with a few letters, then working up to five a week and more. I followed up every letter, told everybody I ever knew that I was looking for a job and followed up every lead.

"Finally I got in to see the editor-in-chief at Parents' Magazine Press. I had written about children's books and I had definite ideas about the direction they should take. He saw my enthusiasm, liked my ideas, and decided to take a chance on me, taking the time to teach me to be an editor in return for the promise he saw. From that job I was able to move on to another with better pay."

Once Margaret was working happily and earning a decent salary, things were eased for Jim. He decided to take time off to study for a master's degree in sociology, something that has enabled him to relate his commercial writing to issues he cares about. It allowed him to leave a straight publicity job for a firm that advises corporations on social problems. For the first time, he was earning a good salary at a job he felt good about. He is now a vice president of the firm.

"Just about the time that Jim got established, my own job situation deteriorated," Margaret relates, "and I felt it was time to move on. I thought that with experience it would be easy to find a new position, but publishing is a competitive industry and the job search took nine long and very difficult months. Again, I told everyone that I was looking. It turned out to be our accountant who heard of an opening in a publishing house and referred me. I was at the right place at the right time when I applied and I got the job. Flukes happen for a reason; I would advise everyone who is job-hunting to reach out in all directions for help. You just never know where the right contact will come from.

"For the moment things are stable in our home. We both have jobs we like and I can afford proper help to care for the children. We realize that we will have to keep working and working hard for the next ten years if we hope to send two children to college, and that there is time in the future for more writing if we want it.

"The important thing is that each of us has been able to help the other to achieve what we really wanted. It would never have happened if I had stayed at home as a dutiful wife trying to conform to my husband's expectations instead of my own needs."

9. You and Your Family

At the beginning of this book, as you began the process of getting to know your self better, your family was mentioned as the possible first source of help and encouragement in your quest.

They are probably also one of your greatest sources of concern.

Every honest working mother admits to some moments of doubt about whether her outside commitment will be harmful to her children. Likewise, almost every wife who considers returning to work after a time at home wonders what the new demands of a job will mean to her marriage relationship.

Sometimes the guilt at the very prospect of taking time and attention away from your family can be great enough to stand in your way, can make you invent obstacles in your job search so that you won't have to wrestle with the problem. Every career counselor is familiar with this ploy—the woman who finds an excuse that makes her back away every time she comes close to making a real change in her life.

Having made the decision that you want and need to work, the time to come to terms with these guilt feelings is now, before you report for a job.

First you must recognize that you can't take on a full-time job and continue doing your same job at home. Working can add a stimulating and personally satisfying new dimension to your life, and your family may actually benefit in many ways. But there is just so much of you to go around. Adding one set of responsibilities means subtracting others. And changing your life inevitably must change the lives of those you live with and love.

You are not going to be able to work all day and still be Little League chauffeur, perfect hostess, head of the church bazaar, and your child's room mother. Your meals are going to become simpler and your family's clothes will become no-iron unless a full-time housekeeper moves in to take your place. How are you going to deal with no longer fulfilling these traditional feminine roles to perfection? How much of your own sense of worth is tied to doing things for others? Are you able to ask your family for the help you're going to need or will you fall into the trap of trying to play Supermother?

You may be able to maintain a better perspective about relinquishing some of your accustomed roles by examining your feelings about what it means to be a woman. Many of us don't even realize how many stereotypes we carry around in our heads until we try to break the mold. But how many of the things you do each day right now are "shoulds"—things you've been conditioned to believe are the job of a mother when they could just as well be done by other members of the family?

Cooking is a perfect example. Anyone who can read and reach the stove is able to learn to cook. Do you just assume that this is somehow your responsibility? Would you be depriving your family of something important if you asked them to begin to share your cooking duties? Or even to settle for cold cuts or fast foods once in a while? Would you be helping them more by staying in the kitchen, or by bringing in a paycheck and supplying them with new ideas, broader horizons, and a new kind of role model?

None of us can totally escape the "shoulds" of our upbringing. They are too deeply ingrained in our psyches. What's more, many of our domestic roles continue to give us pleasure, and we regret sincerely having to relinquish them. But if you want to work, you are going to have to make some changes and compromises, and you must understand that you are not harming your family by changing some of their accustomed patterns.

One of the ways to keep the guilt to a manageable minimum is to talk honestly with your family ahead of time about why you want to work and what it will mean to them, suggests Hunter's Dr. Nancy Stevens. "Working will mean giving up some of the things you have been doing for them. All the members of the family need to explore their feelings and expectations and to share honestly their reservations so that the changes will be the least disruptive for everyone. It's important for a mother to be able to communicate her needs and to get feedback about which areas the family feels are most important for her to maintain. Both husband and children need to know that you share their concern at changing familiar routines, that they still mean as much to you as ever even though you need to take on a new role outside the family. That knowledge means a lot."

"Children can make you feel unnecessarily guilty if you let them, cautions a mother who's gone through the adjustments of a new job. "They're used to having you at their beck and call, and let's face it—youngsters can be selfish.

"What helps is an honest reappraisal of your routines. After all, you are not abandoning your family. You are restructuring your time. First, you have to get it through your head that your physical presence isn't going to solve all your children's conflicts and needs. Then look at your actual everyday schedule. When I did that, I found that most days I actually spent less than three hours a day in the same room with my children, and we shared some of that period with the TV set. The rest of the time they were in their rooms or out with friends or at school. What seemed valuable to me were the short periods of time we would be losing in the afternoon when I was alone with each child. So I decided to reschedule those times, to allot a half hour to each child while they helped me prepare dinner or later in the evening. It doesn't sound important, but it made a big difference to them to know they would still be sure of having my undivided attention for some time every day. It was a kind of extra reassurance that they weren't going to lose me totally because I had a job."

Almost every mother shares concern for the "three-o'clock syndrome," the notion that a mother should be at home to hand out milk and cookies when school is over. But realistically, are your children going to suffer if someone else they know and like is there instead of you, or if they are busy in a happy group situation? The important thing is not to wait until you have a job and are under pressure. Make arrangements for sitters or day-care centers before you leave, give the children a fair amount of time to adjust to their own new routine, and there should be no serious problem when you do disappear.

When your children do make you feel guilty—and they probably will—by telling you how much they miss having you around, stop, before you dissolve with remorse, to consider reality. Isn't it just possible they will benefit from a little more self-reliance and flexibility, a bit more concern for the needs of others? Let them voice their feelings, understand and sympathize with them, but let them know your feelings as well, and the necessity for what you are doing with your life. Keep your own perspective. Remember that change, even positive change, takes time to get used to.

When it comes to practical problems such as rides and errands you can no longer provide for them, there are almost always ways to work out the things that really matter in advance. A neighbor or friend may be willing to take over some of your daytime driving in return for your providing extra rides in the evening, or you may be able to hire a reliable older teen-ager to drive for you.

On the other hand, your children will have to become more selective about their activities. It may no longer be possible to play after school with friends who live beyond biking distance. And more than one family has discovered that the kids don't need or miss many of the meetings, practices, and lessons that kept mother behind the wheel all afternoon. It's often a welcome relief to pare down to the things they really care about.

That applies to you as well as to your children. Your time is going to be very much more limited, your free time woefully precious. You can't say "Yes" to every worthy cause or committee, can't accept every social invitation. You're going to have to pick and choose, putting your energy where it means the most to you. Like the kids, you'll likely discover that you hardly miss many of the time fillers that have been occupying your days.

Begin right now to learn to share your home responsibilities. Try letting your family sit down together to set up a rotating schedule for chores. Make it a rule to stop doing things that others can do themselves. If the kids can get to the library or a shopping center, there's no reason why they can't take care of some of their own errands. Your husband may be able to take over if you've been in charge of the family car, and can probably pitch in with grocery shopping as well.

However helpful your family may be, in most cases it remains mother who is the manager of the household even though she is now away from nine to five every day. Just a little thought and reorganization of your routines can do a lot to help you accomplish more in less time. Try some "systems analysis" in your own home. Begin to plan your needs ahead of time. Keep a list and consolidate your shopping and errands into one trip a week. Plan menus ahead of time so that you don't run out of ingredients before the week is out.

Learn to use odd fragments of time you had previously wasted. Instead of idly leafing through magazines while the children are at the dentist or the barber shop, use the minutes to mark off some of the items on your ever-present errands list. Take advantage of the telephone for staples, items on sale—even birthday and Christmas gifts. Start cooking in double portions, freezing one meal for later use. There are countless ways to work more efficiently at home, and you should be starting to streamline your routines now, before you go to work.

Every working woman agrees that a supportive husband is her best ally. But gaining this support may require your understanding of the real distress many men feel at changes in their familiar home routine.

"Rationally, my husband was all for my working," one woman reports, "but emotionally it was quite an adjustment for him. He was losing his spot as the sole center of my life. For the first time I had obligations that might come before his needs. I was making new demands on him for help at home. And I think he was truly afraid that I might find my new life more interesting than my old one, that he might lose me. He was threatened and needed reassurance. I'd tell any woman just returning to work that it is important to remember how your husband may be feeling while you are all wrapped up in the excitement of change and perhaps are more tired than usual when you get home. If you let him know both before and after you begin to work that he matters to you more than ever, that you need him more than ever, it's likely to help him feel more supportive."

However, awareness and reassurance are not the same thing as overreacting from guilt, a common reflex according to Olga Silverstein of the Ackerman Institute for Family Therapy, herself a homemaker who went back to school at age forty to begin a new career. "Even husbands with the best of intentions can find subtle ways to bring on guilt," she cautions. "After all, a husband has a right to be upset. You are changing the premise of your original marriage contract.

"It is easier to deal with feelings that are right out in the open, with the man who says, 'Do what you want, just see that my dinner is ready on time.' It's the double messages that are more difficult—for instance, when he encourages you to go ahead with your career plans, then wonders out loud to friends how the children are going to manage with no mother at home to look after them. Or the message may not be verbal at all. He may simply go around looking depressed or come up with psychosomatic illnesses that require your time and attention.

"One reaction when a husband—or a child—makes you feel uncomfortable and guilty is to try to become Superwoman, to make up for getting something for yourself by doing all you ever did at home and more. But this simply does not work. The more you try to do, the more you are expected to do. Inevitably this brings on resentment that is harmful to your relationships.

"Nor can you go backward, giving up your own goals, without feeling even more serious resentment. The only answer is to realize that your family's reactions are normal, to understand what is happening, and to sympathize, but to realize that you can't do anything to help your family with these necessary adjustments, that you don't *have* to do anything. Their feelings are legitimate, but so are your needs. New patterns must be worked out. You will not solve the dilemma by trying to overcompensate for your decision to work."

This is not easy advice to follow for women who have been conditioned to plan their lives around other people's needs. Finding the courage to assert yourself, to ask for consideration and help from others, requires a growing sense of your own worth, the knowledge that your needs are important and that your place in your home should not rest solely on serving others.

It is unrealistic to think that you can change your own life without creating changes in your home life. Keep in mind, however, that causing a temporary upset ultimately may bring about a better situation. The status quo is not necessarily the best of all worlds. It is just comfortable to everyone because it is familiar.

But never asking for anything for yourself for fear of making waves is not likely to lead to healthy personal relationships. By making yourself a happier and more fulfilled person, you may strengthen your marriage in the long run. Even the children who complain about the loss of pampering they have enjoyed are likely, as they grow older, to respect you more for your ambitions. Ultimately everyone can benefit from a more stimulated—hence more stimulating—wife and mother.

The Time to Begin

Since *Passages* made the best-seller lists with its message of predictable stages and crises of life, we have become increasingly aware that our fast-moving world does not permit anyone to remain in a fixed state for long. Whether we want it or not, change comes at us from all sides today, and we must be ready to adapt to new needs and options as our lives pass into new stages.

Dr. Paul Seton, director of the Student Counseling Service at Smith College, notes that while the identity crises of adolescence, middle age, and aging have received a considerable amount of attention, another crucial period of crisis occurs "in that decade of the early thirties to early forties . . . when a woman who has married . . . and has reared a family . . . begins to wonder what she is going to do with the second half of her life."

At a Smith seminar for alumni called "Toward Considering a Second Life," Dr. Seton observed that this period of "individuation" is frequently a lonely and difficult one for women who find themselves with a husband and children for whom they are the "prime supplier in terms of emotional nurture."

"There is little societal support for a woman who thinks about redefining herself and her goals at this point," Dr. Seton said. "Moreover, any move she makes in this direction will force the network of people and family dependent on her to redefine themselves, which is bound to cause some dislocation." He stressed that despite the "serious and sometimes grave disruptions" this new self-definition may cause, women owe it to themselves and to others to seek the kind of self-knowledge that will allow them to make, rather than ignore or sidestep, the decisions that control their lives. Redefining oneself during this period is "evidence of maturity and soundness. It is not selfish. [And not doing so] will only mean that you inflict your own discontent, bitterness, and frustration on others."

The years of motherhood, which used to span a woman's most productive years, have shrunk in an era of smaller families spaced closer together in age. Most women today have twenty-five productive years left after their children are grown. So many who continue to value the very important rewards of being a wife and mother have come to realize that this is not a "permanent job;" that they need more of an outlet for their minds and talents now and will need increasingly more as their children grow and leave home. They know they must plan now for the next passage of their lives, to give focus to the future rather than passively waiting for it to happen to them. The families who love them are beginning to learn how to adjust and rearrange to make it possible for women to widen their world.

It's all still new for women, this notion of shaping our own lives and asking our families to conform. We are more comfortable still bending to the needs of others. It may be easier for our daughters who have grown up expecting to combine the demands of a career with motherhood—and who will have this generation as the role models that are missing today.

Meanwhile, we can't afford to wait. We are going to have to take the risks of changing course, joining the growing wave of "late bloomers" who are finding new directions for the second phase of their grown-up lives.

You have devoted years to your family, given your children a good start. Now it is time to add to your world, to find a place outside your home. It will mean changing some of the routines both you and your family have valued, but hopefully replacing them with new kinds of benefits. As you prepare to "re-enter," be heartened to know how many women just like you have already made this transition, have changed their lives and themselves, found new self-pride and satisfaction in their work—and declared the rewards well worth the sacrifice.

Appendix

A. Career Counseling

The benefits of professional counseling in setting career goals cannot be overemphasized. But ironically, the very explosion of these services can lead to a dilemma. If there are several workshops and courses available in your area, how do you decide which is best for you?

Cost is definitely not a valid criterion. Many of the lower-priced offerings at colleges and nonprofit agencies are just as skillfully put together and run as those given by firms that are in the business of career counseling. And a group situation is often more valuable for re-entry women than more expensive one-to-one counseling.

Here are some guidelines for making an educated choice among counseling options, a consensus gathered from a wide range of practicing career counselors:

COUNSELOR CREDENTIALS. Not everyone running career-guidance programs is really qualified to do so. Does the leader have a counseling degree? How many years of experience does the counselor have at this kind of work—and how much experience working with re-entry women?

SIZE OF THE GROUP. Most counselors feel that fifteen is a maximum, ten an ideal for the most effective group interaction and support.

GOALS. Be clear about what this program promises to accomplish. Where does it expect to get you? Will you come out with more self-knowledge? Specific career goals? Wider knowledge of potential careers? Knowledge of the local job market? Job-search skills? Enhanced decision-making ability? More assertiveness? Different workshops serve different needs. You may need more than one to accomplish your goals. Be sure that the program you choose does cover as many of your concerns as possible.

AVAILABILITY OF INDIVIDUAL COUNSELING. Better programs give you the opportunity to consult individually with your counselor for personal attention in addition to your group participation.

FOLLOW-UP. Are the resources of the sponsoring organization still available to you after your workshop or course is over? Can you use their reference materials? Can you return for additional counseling if necessary?

CONNECTION WITH THE JOB MARKET. Many counselors who may be skilled at personal evaluation and skills analysis have little firsthand experience with the actual job market. If you need specific career information and job-hunting advice, be sure your group has contact with employers and working women as resources, that your leader is familiar with the local employment picture.

TESTING. Though many counselors find testing less important than interest and motivation for mature job seekers, most programs do include tests. You should compare how many and what types of tests you will receive for your money.

REFERENCES. Ask for several names of alumni whom you may contact personally for their impressions of the program.

If the offerings in your locality do not meet all of these criteria, they can still be extremely helpful to you. Almost any kind of directed counseling will aid you to focus better on your skills, to gain perspective, and to increase your knowledge of job-hunting techniques. Even when a particular workshop does not offer all of the elements you need, it should point up the kinds of information you will require next and offer resources for finding it. And the positive reinforcement of sharing this experience with a group cannot be overemphasized. It helps so much to know you are not alone in your concerns.

The best counseling is not hand-holding. A good counselor will expect and demand that you do most of the work yourself, with guidance, so that you learn about yourself in the process. Ultimately, the decisions you make, the energy and drive required to launch a new career, must be your own. No one can do these things for you. But counseling is a constructive and valuable start.

Here is a state-by-state listing of various counseling services and re-entry programs. Those who answered questionnaires are followed by their descriptions of the services they provide. This is not a comprehensive list by any means. Use these names as referrals to check further into what is available in your locality.

ALABAMA

University of Alabama Counseling Center
University, AL 35486
(205) 348-6560

Offers individual counseling, group programs, testing, referral services, and a research library. Has offered career exploration workshops. Free.

ARIZONA

Job Search Skills Project
Women's Center
1129 N. 1st Street
Phoenix, AZ 85004
(602) 258-9948

Pilot program for state, offering forty-hour course on career awareness, job-search skills, consciousness raising, assertiveness. Sliding fees.

University of Arizona
1717 E. Speedway, Room 3214
Tucson, AZ 85719
(602) 626-3902

Offers individual counseling, group programs, and referral. "Phase"

project under Opportunities for Women Section of Division of Continuing Education provides counseling, job readiness, and job development for displaced homemakers. Free.

Other suggested sources of information: *Tucson Women's Commission; Arizona Women's Commission; Women's Studies Department, University of Arizona.*

ARKANSAS

University of Arkansas Student Development Center
202 D University Hall, University of Arkansas
Fayetteville, AR 72701
(501) 575-3553

Offers individual counseling, group programs, testing and referral services, assertiveness training, and support groups. Free.

Other suggested sources of information: *Women's Center Ozark Guidance Center, Springdale Commission on the Needs of Women.*

CALIFORNIA

A statewide directory of California women's organizations is available from Jayne Townsend & Associates, 30 Hotaling Place, San Francisco, CA 94111.
(415) 986-3105. $1.25.

For a directory of Santa Clara County resources for women, write to Re-entry Program, San Jose State University, San Jose, CA 95192. Free.

Advocates for Women, Inc.
256 Sutter Street
San Francisco, CA 94108
(415) 391-4870

Also branches at:
2054 University Avenue, Suite 500
Berkeley, CA 94704

22630 Foothill Boulevard
Hayward, CA 94541

Job listings and career-resource library open to all. Primarily an economic development center offering workshops and individual counseling to CETA-eligible women with job training in nontraditional areas. Also sponsors a women-in-management training program.

Publications include *The Résumé,* a guide to résumé development, 75¢ plus 25¢ mailing charge; *Your Job Rights,* a booklet on employment resources in San Francisco, including career counseling, interview procedures, hiring, and promotional practices; 50¢ plus 25¢ mailing charge.

Career Planning Center, Inc.
1631 S. La Cienega Boulevard
Los Angeles, CA 90035
(313) 277-6633

Pioneering office as transitional agency for re-entering women and advocate for alternative work patterns.

Provides vocational information, career planning and development, job referral, training. Offers work-experience programs, on-the-job-training programs for older and economically disadvantaged women, displaced-homemaker services, career education. Free except for special workshops.

New Ways to Work
457 Kingsley Avenue
Palo Alto, CA 94301
(415) 321-9675

Also:
149 Ninth Street
San Francisco, CA 94103
(415) 552-2949

Promotes innovative job patterns, offers job-sharing counseling and training. Also individual counseling, group workshops. Sliding fees, maximum $8 yearly for use of job listings, one counseling session, one brainstorming session. Workshops have additional fees. Many publications on job sharing, alternative work patterns; write for publications list.

Resource Center for Women
445 Sherman Avenue
Palo Alto, CA 94306
(415) 324-1710

Offers individual counseling, testing, referral services, research library, employment information. Active link to educational and vocational opportunities in the Bay Area; $15 per year membership, $15 per hour for counseling.

Woman's Way
710 C Street, Suite 1
San Rafael, CA 94901
(415) 453-4494

Counseling, career workshops, job listings, network of Bay Area employers for informational interviewing, taped interviews with a variety of women workers, extensive library on careers and Bay Area opportunities, special information on nontraditional careers, CETA outreach program. Sliding fees for counseling and workshops, no fee for library or CETA programs.

Women in Apprenticeship Program, Inc.
25 Taylor Street, Room 617
San Francisco, CA 94102
(415) 673-3925

Counseling, testing, tutoring, and a research library to help women interested in apprenticeship into the skilled trades.

Women's Center
University of California, Berkeley
Building T-9
Berkeley, CA 94720
(415) 642-4286

Offers individual counseling, group programs, referral services, a research library. Free. Publications include *Is Berkeley the Right Place for You?,* a guide for prospective re-entry women.

Other sources of information:

Center for New Directions
7112 Owensmouth Avenue
Canonga Park, CA
(213) 347-5480

Mills College
Center for Career Planning
Oakland, CA 94613
(415) 632-2700, ext. 216

UCLA Women's Resource Center
2 Dodd Hall
UCLA
Los Angeles, CA 90024
(213) 825-3945

CONNECTICUT

FACES (Fairfield Adult Career and Education Services)
Fairfield University
1561 North Benson Road
Fairfield, CT 06430
(203) 255-5411, ext. 681

Individual and group counseling, testing, referral service, research library, workshops. Drop-in services free; various fees.

Information and Counseling Service for Women
301 Crown Street
New Haven, CT 06520
(203) 436-8242

Individual and group counseling, employment services.

Norwalk Community College
Counseling Center
333 Wilson Avenue
Norwalk, CT 06854
(203) 853-2040

Individual and group counseling, referral service, research library, workshops.

Career and Educational Counseling Center
Stamford, YWCA
422 Summer Street
Stamford, CT
(203) 348-7727

Individual and group counseling, testing, workshops. $20 for up to three counseling sessions, $10 per test, fees for special workshops.

Office of Placement & Career Planning
Box U-51
University of Connecticut
Storrs, CT 06268
(203) 486-3013

COLORADO

Denver Women's Career Center
1665 Grant Street
Denver, Colorado 80203
(303) 861-7254

Small group sessions followed by individual counseling. Testing, career information library and Denver labor market information. $150. First class free.

DISTRICT OF COLUMBIA

Wider Opportunities for Women, Inc.
1649 K Street, NW
Washington, D.C. 20006
(202) 638-4868

Employment resource center for women now in its 14th year. Individual and group counseling, workshops, support groups, resource library, information on local job market, job listings. Center privileges $20 per month; ACT (Active Career Techniques) series, $75 for two months. CETA training programs and pilot programs for older women, special fees for workshops.

DELAWARE

Info
2800 Pennsylvania Avenue
Wilmington, DE 19806
(302) 571-8100

Educational/vocational training, career counseling and information-referrals statewide with toll-free number for Delaware residents. Free.

Access
Division of Continuing Education
University of Delaware
John M. Clayton Hall
Newark, DE 19711
(302) 738-2741

Also:
Dover AFB
Dover, DE
(302) 678-5310

Wilcastle Center
Wilmington, DE
(302) 738-7741

Educational and career counseling, career search workshops and courses, testing, occupational consultants. Orientation workshops and skills refreshers for new adult students. Free.

FLORIDA

Career Resource Center
University of Florida
G-22, Reitz Union
Gainesville, FL 32611
(904) 392-1601

Individual and group counseling, referral services, research library, minicourses on second careers, audio-visual career information, workshops for women on job-interview techniques. Open to all, but principally intended for students. Free.

Center for Continuing Education for Women
Valencia Community College
P.O. Box 3028
Orlando, FL 32802
(813) 299-5000, ext. 526

Major educational brokering service in the area. Individual and group counseling, testing, referrals, research library. Displaced homemaker services, job club. Counseling free; small fee for testing.

Other suggested sources of information:

Center for the Continuing Education of Women
Miami-Dade Community College
300 Northeast Second Avenue
Miami, FL 33540
(305) 685-4374

GEORGIA

Educational Information and Referral Service
Lenox Square Professional Concourse
3393 Peachtree Road NE
Atlanta, GA 30326
(404) 233-7497

IDAHO

Career Planning and Placement Center
University of Idaho
Moscow, ID 83843
(208) 885-6121

Offers referral and research library to students, alumni. Free.

ILLINOIS

Women's Employment Resource Directory for Greater Chicago Area
(including counseling services) available free from Adult Career Advocate Program, School of Education, Northwestern University, Evanston, IL 60201.

Also available: *Pathfinder,* a back-to-school guide for adults covering the Chicago metropolitan area, with a section on counseling services. Order from The Program for Women, Northwestern University, 619 Emerson Street, Evanston, IL 60201. $1.50.

Adult Re-Entry Programs and Services
Triton College
2000 Fifth Avenue
River Grove, IL 60171
(312) 456-0300

Offers educational and vocational counseling, testing, life-planning, and career-exploration courses, preview seminars for adults considering enrollment, career workshops, many aids, including support groups and skills refreshers for returning students, child-care facilities. Free counseling and testing, varying fees for courses and workshops, but all are moderate.

Career Path Workshop
125 North Marion
Oak Park Mall
Oak Park, IL 60301
(312) 848-9210

Three-session re-entry workshops, $45; career library. Videotaped interview practice.

DePaul University
25 East Jackson Boulevard
Chicago, IL 60604
(312) 321-7694

Re-entry and life-planning workshops, special adult counseling and advising.

Elgin Community College
1700 Spartan Drive
Elgin, IL 60120
(312) 697-1000, ext. 220

Re-entry program, counseling, testing, referral at main college and five outreach campuses.

Flexible Careers
37 South Wabash Avenue
Room 703
Chicago, IL 60603
(312) 236-6028

Nonprofit career consultation service with extensive research files including taped interviews with women in varied occupations, "people network" of professionals who will serve as information sources for newcomers, individual and group counseling for self-assessment, job-search skills; $30 registration fee includes all reference resources plus two counseling sessions within a two-month period.

Mundelein College
6363 North Sheridan
Chicago, IL 60660
(312) 262-8100, ext. 333

Individual and group counseling, testing, referral, research library, stress on skills identification for returning homemakers (students and alumnae). Weekend college, flexible courses.

INDIANA

Career Center
Indiana University
Bloomington, IN 47405
(812) 337-1526

Counseling, workshops, testing, research library, referral services for students and alumni. Free except for specialized courses.

Center for Women
Division of Continuing Studies
Indiana-Purdue University
1301 E. 38th Street
Indianapolis, IN 46205
(317) 923-1231, ext. 287

Assists women back to work or to school through personal and group counseling, testing, referral services, research library; $15 for three sessions, including testing.

Continuing Education for Women
Bloomington, IN 47405
(813) 337-1684

Individual and group counseling, referral service, research library, a returning women's support group and newsletter, noncredit programming for returning women in communities throughout the state; $15 for three sessions, including testing.

IOWA

Community Career Planning Center for Women
Drake University
1158 27th Street
Des Moines, IA 50311
(515) 271-2916

Individual and group counseling, workshops, testing, referral services, research library, job listings, displaced-homemaker services, financial-aid information. Counseling free, testing $15, varying fees for workshops.

Project Re-Entry
Division of Women's Programs
College for Continuing Education
Drake University
2700 University Avenue
Des Moines, IA 50311
(515) 271-2181

Nine-month internship program including workshops, counseling, personal assessment, placement in local businesses, mentor program. Participating employers pay stipend to cover fee.

Women's Resource and Action Center
130 N. Madison Street
Iowa City, IA
(319) 353-6265

Counseling, support groups,
brown-bag luncheons for women
students at the University of Iowa.
Special services for women returning
to school. Free.

KANSAS

For information/referral services call
toll-free: (800) 532-6772.

Adult Life Resource Center
University of Kansas
Division of Continuing Education
1246 Mississippi Avenue, Annex A
Lawrence, KS 66044
(913) 864-4794

Focus is to help adults, particularly
women, with life-cycle changes,
offering counseling, testing,
educational advice, workshops,
publications career library.
Counseling and testing fee, $15;
workshop fees vary. Workshops
offered around the state.

*Emily Taylor Women's Resource
and Career Center*
218 Strong Hall
University of Kansas
Lawrence, KS 66045
(913) 864-3552

Counseling referral, research library,
support groups, principally for
students but not restricted. Free.

KENTUCKY

*University of Kentucky Counseling
Center*
Lexington, KY 40506
(606) 258-8701

Individual and group counseling,
testing, study-skills refreshers, math
anxiety groups for returning
students. Free.

LOUISIANA

Newcomb Women's Center
1229 Broadway
New Orleans, LA 70118
(504) 865-4424

Counseling, limited testing, career
research library for re-entering
students. Free.

Other suggested sources of
information: *Loyola Women's Center,
Delgado Women's Center, WYES-TV*
("Opportunities" program for
women).

MARYLAND

Women's Guide to Baltimore
published annually, available free
from Women's Resource and
Advocacy Center, 12 East 25th
Street, Baltimore, MD 21218.

Baltimore New Directions for Women
12 East 25th Street
Baltimore, MD 21218
(301) 889-6677

Also:

*Career Counseling Center/Training
Institute*
2517 North Charles Street
Baltimore, MD 21218
(301) 566-8570

Multifaceted agency offering
individual and group counseling,
job-search workshops, information
on education and employment
opportunities, resource library,
program for nontraditional careers.
Sliding fees.

Center for Displaced Homemakers
2435 Maryland Avenue
Baltimore, MD 21218
(301) 243-5000

New Phase: Career Readiness Center for Women
50 Monroe Street
Rockville, MD 20850
(301) 279-1800

Comprehensive individual and group counseling, referrals, research library, workshops. Free.

Program for Returning Students
University of Maryland
Shoemaker Building
College Park, MD 20742
(301) 454-2935

Individual and group counseling, testing and referral services, special courses, orientation and workshops in study skills for returning students. Free.

Women's Management Development Project
Goucher College
Towson, MD 21204
(301) 825-3300

Re-entry internship program focusing on management skills. Tuition, $2,000.

MASSACHUSETTS

Career Development Office
Smith College
Northampton, MA 01063
(413) 584-2700

Offers alumnae annual "second life" seminars for considering use of their time, talents, and energy as family responsibilities lighten.

Career Services Office
Mount Holyoke College
South Hadley, MA 01075
(413) 538-2080

Alumnae are offered job listings newsletter, career advisers' network of graduates who will provide resource information on their field of work.

Civic Center and Clearing House
14 Beacon Street
Boston, MA 02108
(617) 227-1762

Career and vocational advisory services, counseling, referrals, research library, job-search skills; $25 per counseling session.

Continuum
785 Centre Street
Newton, MA 02158
(617) 964-3322

Career education program for women over thirty combining an academic year with three work internships; about $2,000.

Educational Opportunity Center
140 Clarendon Street
Boston, MA 02116
(617) 536-7940, ext. 34 or 35

Branches in Lynn, Springfield, Worcester, and New Bedford.

Educational counseling service provides testing, application, and financial-aid assistance. Free.

Project Re-Entry
c/o Civic Center
and Clearing House
14 Beacon Street
Boston, MA 02108
(617) 227-1762

Structured internship and counseling program for re-entering women; $750.

Radcliffe Alumni Career Service
10 Garden Street
Cambridge, MA 02138
(617) 495-8631

Counseling, workshops, referral, research library, career panels. Support groups for job hunters; $5 registration fee for nonalumnae; varying fees for workshops.

Women's Educational and Industrial Union
356 Boylston Street
Boston, MA 02116
(617) 536-5651

Individual counseling, workshops, career resource library, placement service; $10 for initial counseling, $5 for subsequent appointments; $20 annual fee for placement services and job-search workshops; $5 for specialized workshops in résumés, interviewing, etc.

YWCA of Boston
140 Clarendon Street
Boston, MA 02116
(617) 536-7940

Employment programs aimed toward disadvantaged, displaced-homemaker program at West Suburban branch, nontraditional job training, job placement, administrative-assistant training. Free or low fees.

MICHIGAN

Career Planning and Placement
University of Michigan
3200 SAB
Ann Arbor, MI 48109
(313) 764-7457

Complete counseling and career services for students and alumni. Annual women's career fair open to all with decision-making workshops for re-entering women on career information, job-hunting strategies, managing multiple roles, interviewing.

Center for Continuing Education for Women
University of Michigan
328–330 Thompson
Ann Arbor, MI 48109
(313) 764-0449

Counseling and information for women dealing with transitions in their lives, job-search workshops, information and referral on education and careers, services and support groups for returning students, refresher courses, "brown bag" lunches, internships in business, government, and within the university, financial aid. No fees.

New Options Personnel
2908 Book Building
Detroit, MI 48226
(313) 961-8337

Individual counseling, skills assessment, presentation skills, community and educational resource referral; $45 first session, $30 for subsequent sessions. Also placement and CETA programs for nontraditional jobs development.

MINNESOTA

Minnesota Women's Center
University of Minnesota
306 Walter Library
117 Pleasant Street SE
Minneapolis, MN 55455
(612) 373-3850

Individual counseling for career, academic/education, personal problems; extensive information and referral resources, workshops, scholarships for returning women students, support groups for returning students. No fee.

Other sources of information:

Career Clinic
Downtown YWCA
1130 Nicollet Avenue
Minneapolis, MN 55403
(612) 332-0501

Career Clinic
North Suburban YWCA
North Hennepin Community College
7411 85th Avenue North
Minneapolis, MN 55445
(612) 425-4541

Community Career Center
Fair Community Education Center
3915 Adair Avenue North
Crystal, MN 55422
(612) 537-6506

Working Opportunities for Women
YWCA Women's Center
65 East Kellogg Boulevard,
Room 437
St. Paul, MN 55101
(612) 227-8401

MISSISSIPPI

Placement and Career Information Center
Mississippi State University
P.O. Drawer P, 316 Union Building
Mississippi State, MS 39762
(601) 325-3344

Individual and group counseling, testing, referral, research library open to all women. Special programs for women. No fees.

MISSOURI

Career Planning and Placement Center
110 Noyer
University of Missouri
Columbia, MO 65211
(314) 882-6801

Counseling, testing, referral, research library, job seekers' support groups. No fee.

Other suggested sources of information: *New Directions Center, McCambridge Center for Women.*

Washington University
Forsyth and Skinker
St. Louis, MO 63130
(314) 889-6759

Workshops, seminars, referral services. Counseling limited to students. Workshop fees, $50 for six to eight sessions.

MONTANA

Focus on Women
Montana State University
Bozeman, MT 59717
(406) 994-2012

Individual and group counseling, testing, referral services, research library, "sack lunch" seminars, outreach program of two-day workshops held throughout the state, three-day annual statewide conference on women's issues. No fees for counseling; some fees for workshops.

NEBRASKA

Counseling Center
Career Placement and Planning
Co-equal Educational Office
University of Nebraska
Lincoln, NE
(402) 472-2213

Individual and group counseling, testing and referral, annual "back to school" informational conference for adults. Free.

NEW JERSEY

Options of Women in New Jersey, a directory of career services and continuing-education opportunities, $5.00 plus $.50 for mailing, published by New Jersey College and University Coalition on Women's Education, Adrienne S. Anderson, Editor, 201 Fells Road, Essex Falls, NJ 07021.

Center for Women
Fairleigh Dickinson University
Madison Avenue
Madison, NJ 07940
(201) 377-4700, ext. 271

Individual counseling, testing, referral service, workshops. Free except for vocational test fee, $5.00.

Douglass Advisory Services for Women
Rutgers Women's Center
Rutgers University
132 George Street
New Brunswick, NJ 08903
(201) 932-9603

Individual and group counseling, testing, referral services, research library; counseling for women interested in returning to school or starting their own business, displaced-homemakers services, outreach center for minority women. No fee for counseling; small fees for workshops and testing.

Women's Center
Montclair State College
Upper Montclair, NJ 07043
(201) 893-5106

Individual and group counseling, referral services, research library. Wednesday noon programs for women. "Second Careers" Program for adults who want to begin or resume study for bachelor's degree.

NEW MEXICO

Financial Aid and Career Services
Mesa Vista Hall 213D
University of New Mexico
Albuquerque, NM
(505) 277-2531

Counseling, testing, referral and research services; miniworkshops, career-decision seminar, computerized guidance information. Free other than testing ($2), placement ($15).

Re-Entry Program
University of New Mexico
1716 Las Lomas NE
(505) 277-5161

Individual and group counseling, testing, referral services. Free.

Other information sources: *New Mexico Commission on the Status of Women,* Plaza Del Sol Building, Albuquerque, NM 87102

NEW YORK

Adult Counseling and Resources Center
New York University
125 Shimkin Hall
50 West 4th Street
New York, NY 10003
(212) 598-2085

Counseling in life planning, skills identification, job/employer research, résumé and interview preparation, workshops for re-entry, math confidence, writing block; Career Resource Collection open daily for research. Varying fees.

Counseling Women
14 East 60th Street
New York, NY 10022
(212) 486-9755

Career-planning workshops,
career-information programs,
lunchtime career forums. Fees for
individual events, $5 to $25;
workshop, $125; five sessions.

*Ellen Morse Tishman Memorial
Seminars*
Hunter College of the City
University of New York
Career Counseling and Placement
Office
695 Park Avenue
New York, NY 10021
(212) 570-5254

Ten-session seminar given twice
yearly for college-educated women
with family responsibilities who are
planning to return to work. Includes
testing, individual counseling, help
with job search, visits from working
women in a variety of fields,
resource library. $150.

Human Relations Center
New School for Social Research
66 West 12th Street
New York, NY 10011
(212) 741-5600

Courses include career planning, job
information, assertiveness training,
internship opportunities. Varying
fees—approximately $40–$75.

Janice LaRouche Assoc. Inc.
333 Central Park West
New York, NY 10025
(212) 663-0970

Workshops also offered at:

New School for Social Research
66 West 12th Street
New York, NY 10011
(212) 741-5600

YWCA
53rd Street and Lexington
Avenue
New York, NY 10022
(212) 755-4500

Workshops in career planning and
job search, assertiveness, job
advancement. Fees vary—approximately $90–$165.

New Options
26 West 56th Street
New York, NY 10019
(212) 541-4114

Self-assessment, life planning,
assertiveness training,
communications skills.

*Regional Learning Service of Central
New York*
405 Oak Street
Syracuse, NY 13203
(315) 425-5262

Individual counseling, referral
services, research library, community
workshops on educational/career
issues. Educational, career, and
job-seeking counseling; $20 for two
months, $10 for one-month renewal.

Other sources of information:
Women's Information Center,
Syracuse YWCA.

Ruth Shapiro Associates
200 East 30th Street
New York, NY 10016
(212) 889-4284

Career development and self-marketing, assertiveness training, from one day, $35, to complete program, $245. Individual counseling —$45 first session, $35 second session.

Vistas for Women
515 North Street—YWCA
White Plains, NY 10605
(914) 949-6227

Individual and group counseling, assertiveness and career-planning groups, job-search workshops. Fees vary; typical workshop, $50–$70.

Womanschool
424 Madison Avenue
New York, NY 10017
(212) 688-4606

Lifetime "Career Systems" program includes career planning and education, certificate programs (career-oriented), job search, career advancement. Varying fees per course—$45–$135.

Women's Career Center, Inc.
121 North Fitzhugh Street
Rochester, NY 14614
(716) 442-8053

Individual and group counseling, referral services, resource network, research library. Fees, $10–$40. Nonprofit career-counseling and referral agency for unemployed and underemployed women.

NORTH CAROLINA

Department of Continuing Education
Duke University
107 Bivins Building
Durham, NC 27708
(919) 684-6259

Peer counseling program assists adults making transitions such as returning to work or school, career planning, goal setting. Referrals for job placement or professional counseling, extensive resource library, file of contacts for informational interviewing. "Center for Lifetime Learning" courses include many facets of career development. Small registration fee for peer counseling, varying fees for courses.

NORTH DAKOTA

Counseling Center
University of North Dakota
Box 8112
University Station
Grand Forks, ND 58202
(701) 777-2127

Individual counseling, interest and aptitude testing, career-information library. No fee.

OHIO

Womenfocus
Lifelong Learning Institute
Cuyahoga Community College
2900 Community College Avenue
Cleveland, OH 44115
(216) 845-4000, ext. 250

Also:
Western Campus
11000 West Pleasant Valley
Parma, OH 44129

Eastern Campus
25444 Harvard Road
Cleveland, OH 44122

Individual and group counseling, testing, referral services; workshops and seminars on personal growth, career exploration, survival in the marketplace, counseling in career and life planning, displaced-homemaker program. No fees for individual counseling; group programs, approximately $25

Other suggested sources of information:

Adult Resource Center
University of Akron
302 East Buchtel—Buchtel Hall 68
Akron, OH 44325
(216) 375-7448

Educational Information Center of Greater Cincinnati
22 Garfield Place
Cincinnati, OH 45202
(513) 241-9333

Lifelong Learning Educational Information Centers
Ohio University
Tupper Hall, Room 302B
Athens, OH 45701

Options:

Adult Career/Education Services, Inc.
96 South Grant Avenue
Columbus, OH 43215
(614) 464-2662

PENNSYLVANIA

Job Advisory Service
Chatham College
Beatty Hall
Woodland Road
Pittsburgh, PA 15212
(412) 441-6660

Individual and group counseling, testing, referral services, research library, displaced-homemaker services. Group programs offered at other local colleges and neighborhood centers. Fees vary—$15–$90.

Options for Women, Inc.
8419 Germantown Avenue
Philadelphia, Pa. 19118
(215) 242 4955
Also in Chestnut Hill and Center City

Career advisory and consulting service, one of the first in the country, offering individual and group programs, testing, and a research library. Fees vary.

Other suggested sources of information:

Adult Career and Education Services
1005 West 3rd Street
Williamsport, PA 17701
(717) 326-3761 ext. 246

Lifelong Learning Center
Free Library of Philadelphia
Logan Square
Philadelphia, PA 19103
(215) 567-4353

Lifelong Learning Center
Reading Public Library
5th and Franklin Streets
Reading, PA 19602
(215) 376-6501

Return
Adult Education and Career Counseling Center
Montgomery County Community College
Walnut and Penn Streets
Pottstown, PA 19464
(215) 323-1939

Return
Continuing Education for Mature Students
Bucks County Community College
Newton, PA 18940
(215) 368-5861

Return
Opportunities/Adults
Delaware County Community
College
Media, PA 19063
(215) 353-5400 ext. 324

RHODE ISLAND

*Rhode Island Career Counseling
Service*
301 Roger Williams Building
22 Hayes Street
Providence, RI 02908
(401) 272-0900

SOUTH CAROLINA

Career Planning Office
University of South Carolina
Columbia, SC
(803) 777-7280

Individual counseling, testing,
referral and research library, alumni
referral network, job-search development workshops. Works principally
with alumni.

TENNESSEE

Adult Resource Center
Memphis State
University–Continuing Education
265 Administration Building
Memphis, TN 38152
(901) 454-4544

TEXAS

*Vocational Guidance Service Division
VGS, Inc.*
2525 San Jacinto
Houston, TX 77002
(713) 659-1800

"Women Work for Work" program
includes counseling, career-
development workshops, testing,
referral services, research library,

placement, support groups for job
seekers, and tours of nontraditional
worksites. Sliding fees according to
income.

UTAH

The Phoenix Institute
383 South 600 East
Salt Lake City, UT 84102
(801) 532-5080

Individual and group counseling,
career information and referral,
placement and follow-up support
groups for women entering
nontraditional employment areas.
Offers services for displaced
homemakers, help with job-search
skills, assertiveness training,
publishes monthly publication for
Utah working women. Fees only for
counseling (no fees for
disadvantaged).

VERMONT

Center for Career Development
University of Vermont
Burlington, VT 05401
(802) 656-3450

Individual and group counseling,
testing, referral services, research
library. Primarily but not exclusively
for alumni and students. No fees.

VIRGINIA

Alternative Careers
816 South Walter Reed Drive
Arlington, VA 22204
(703) 920-8357

Individual and group counseling,
testing, referral services, research
library; self-help center for career
planning and job development.
Offers career search series, internship
programs, workshops at various
locations. Single sessions, $5–$12.

Women's Resource Center
University College
University of Richmond
Richmond, VA 23173
(804) 285-6316

Individual and group counseling, testing, referral services, research library, help with educational, personal, re-entry, concerns of adult women, peer counseling, women's exchange discussion groups. Fees vary—peer counseling, $5 per hour; classes, $35–40; life-planning seminar course, $200.

Other sources:

Northern Virginia Community College
Annandale Campus
8922 Little River Turnpike
Fairfax, VA 22030
(703) 323-3200

Northern Virginia Information and Counseling Center for Women
127 Park Street NE, Suite A
Vienna, VA 22180
(703) 281-2657

WASHINGTON

Employment Resources for Women in Seattle available from Seattle Department of Human Resources, 400 Yester, Seattle, WA 98104.

Women's Directory for the Puget Sound Area available from Pandora, 434 Northeast 72nd, Seattle, WA 98115.

Career and Life Planning
University of Washington/
Continuing Education
1209 Northeast 41st Street
Seattle, WA 98105
(206) 543-4262

Individual counseling, testing, group programs, referral services, research library, special peer counselor training and services. Counseling, $20 per session; workshops, $25–$125.

Individual Development Center, Inc.
1020 East John Street
Seattle, WA 98102
(206) 329-0600

Individual and group counseling, testing, referral services, research library. Offers help with career and life planning, decision-making, stress management, job-search skills; also works with companies and individuals for career development and advancement; $30 per hour for counseling, $50–$85 for seminar workshops.

WEST VIRGINIA

Placement Service
West Virginia University
Mountain Lair
Morgantown, WV 26506
(304) 293-2221

Individual and group counseling, referral services, research library. Free.

Other suggested sources of information:

Women's Information Center
West Virginia University
Morgantown, WV 26506
(304) 293-2221

WISCONSIN

A listing of women's centers in Wisconsin is available from Women's Education Resources, University of Wisconsin Extension, 428 Lowell Hall, 610 Langdon, Madison, WI 53706.

*Community-based Educational
Counseling for Adults*
University of Wisconsin—Extension
432 North Lake Street
Madison, WI 53706
(608) 263-2055

Contact for addresses and numbers
of local counseling sites in fifty
counties.

Counseling and Guidance Clinic
Education Building
University of Wisconsin
Madison, WI 53706
(608) 262-9461

Offers counseling, testing, and
referral services; $4 fee charged only

for test scoring. Training center of
doctoral and masters students at the
university department of counseling
and guidance.

Research Center on Women
3401 South 39th
Milwaukee, WI 53214
(414) 671-5400

Individual and group counseling,
testing, referral services, research
library. Testing, counseling session,
access to career information and job
listings, $25; follow-up counseling
sessions, $15. "Making Alternative
Plans" is a group counseling
program for women exploring
options.

B. Sources of Additional Information

Catalyst
14 East 60th Street
New York, NY 10022

A national nonprofit organization dedicated to helping women choose, launch, and advance their careers. Catalyst offers a wealth of helpful printed information, an extensive up-to-the-minute reference library on all phases of women and work, and maintains a network of career-resource centers for women. Write for free publications list. Among the materials currently available are:

List of Catalyst National Network, more than 100 local resource centers listed by states. Free.

Résumé Preparation Manual, a step-by-step guide. $4.95.

Planning for Work, a self-guidance workbook. $1.75.

Your Job Campaign, a job-search guide. $1.75.

Career Opportunities Series, separate publications on fields including accounting, advertising, art, banking, communications, counseling, data processing, education, engineering, environmental affairs, finance, fund raising, health services, home economics, insurance, law, library service, personnel, psychology, public relations, publishing, real estate, recreation, retailing, social work, travel, and urban planning. $1.50 each. (On orders under $5, please include 50¢ for postage and handling.)

Displaced Homemakers
Information Business and
Professional Women's Foundation
2012 Massachusetts Avenue NW
Washington, DC 20036

Approximately twenty-five states so far have passed measures to provide assistance to displaced homemakers, women over thirty-five who, through divorce, separation, widowhood, or other crises in midlife, have been displaced from their primary job of homemaker and forced into the labor market with little training. The Washington address is a clearing-house for information and referral to local centers in ten regions across the country. Many programs of counseling and job training are presently in operation.

Merchandising Your Job Talents
U. S. Department of Labor
Employment and Training
Administration
Washington, DC 20213

Concise guide to self-appraisal, preparing a résumé and letter of application, and job-interview techniques. Free.

National Center for Educational Brokering
Office for Research and Publishing
405 Oak Street
Syracuse, NY 13203

Numerous publications on education and educational counseling. Write for free publications list.

Directory: Educational and Career Information Services for Adults (including listing of state directors of educational information). $2.

C. Educational Programs for Mature Students

CLEP (College Level Examination Program) Test Centers and other participating institutions. Free.
CLEP Registration Guide. Free.
CLEP General and Subject Examinations. $1.00 each.

The College Board
Box 1824
Princeton, NJ 08541

College Learning, Anytime, Anywhere
by Ewald Nyquist, Jack Arbolino, and Gene Hawes
Harcourt Brace Jovanovich, Inc.
757 Third Avenue
New York, NY 10017

Continuing Education Programs and Services for Women
Women's Bureau
U. S. Department of Labor
Washington, DC 20210
$.70

Get Credit for What You Know
Women's Bureau
U. S. Department of Labor
Washington, DC 20210
Free.

National Directory of External Degree Programs by
Alfred Munzert
Hemisphere Publications
Distributed by Hawthorn Books
260 Madison Avenue
New York, NY 10016

NATTS Directory
National Association of Trade and Technical Schools
2021 L Street NW
Washington, DC 20036

Listing of more than four hundred schools cross-referenced by field and location, approved by the national association, and recognized by the U. S. Office of Education. Courses range from acting and advertising art to watch-making and X-ray skills. Free.

The New York Times *Guide to Continuing Education in America* (prepared by the College Entrance Examination Board)
Quadrangle Press
330 Madison Avenue
New York, NY 10017

D. Financial Aid for Education

Educational Financial Aid Sources for Women
Clairol Loving Care Scholarship Program
345 Park Avenue, 5th floor
New York, NY 10022

Information on Clairol scholarships and nine other programs for women, with reference sources for additional information. Free.

Financial Aid: A Partial List of Resources for Women
The Project on the Status and Education of Women
Association of American Colleges
1818 R Street NW
Washington, DC 20009

Extensive listing of scholarship programs, general and specialized, including a number directed to mature women or returning students. Includes extensive resource bibliography. Free.

Scholarships
Scholarships Department
Business and Professional Women's Foundation
2012 Massachusetts Avenue NW
Washington, DC 20036

Information on four programs available to women over age twenty-five to upgrade skills or complete education. Free.

A Selected List of Major Fellowship Opportunities and Aids to Advanced Education for United States Citizens
Fellowship Office
Commission on Human Resources
National Research Counsel
2101 Constitution Avenue
Washington, DC 20418

A Selected List of Post-secondary Education Opportunities for Minorities and Women
U. S. Department of Health, Education, and Welfare
Office of Bureau of Higher Education
400 Maryland Avenue SW
Washington, DC 20202

Student Consumer's Guide: 6 Federal Financial Aid Programs
U. S. Department of Health, Education and Welfare
Office of Education
400 Maryland Avenue SW
Washington, DC 20202

E. Career Information

Catalyst Career Opportunities Series
(*see* page 169)

Careers for Women
The Women's Bureau
U. S. Department of Labor
Washington, DC 20210

A series of individual pamphlets on medical technology, urban planning, engineering, pharmacology, mathematics, technical writing, personnel, and trade apprenticeships. Free.

I'm Madly in Love with Electricity
... and Other Comments About
Their Work by Women in Science
and Engineering
Attn: Careers
Lawrence Hall of Science
University of California
Berkeley, CA 94720
$2; make check or money order payable to Regents, University of California.

Math/Science Network
Math/Science Resource Center
Mills College
Oakland, CA 94613

Contact for informational materials on work and study in math-based fields, contacts with women working in these fields.

Medicine: A Woman's Career
American Medical Women's
Association
1740 Broadway
New York, NY 10019

Advice on educational preparation, medical curricula requirements, and sources of financial aid. $1.

Recruiting Women for Traditionally
"Male" Careers
Project on the Status and Education of Women
Association of American Colleges
1818 R Street NW
Washington, DC 20009
Free.

Discusses careers for women in medicine, dentistry, veterinary medicine, law, engineering, science, and math, with extensive listings of further sources of information.

Resource Directory for Women
Moving Up
Attn: Careers
Lawrence Hall of Science
University of California
Berkeley, CA 94720

For women interested in science and technology, information on SanFrancisco Bay Area resource women, educational programs, companies employing people in science and engineering, opportunities for volunteer internships. Free.

Wanted by the Law: Women
Boalt Hall Women's Association
School of Law
University of California
Berkeley, CA 94720

Describes various specializations in the law, details about application and admissions procedures; deals with the unique problems of the older woman applying to law school. Free.

A Woman's Guide to Apprenticeship
Women's Bureau
U. S. Department of Labor
Washington, DC 20210

Guide to opportunities in the skilled trades. Free.

Women and Health Careers: A Guide for Career Exploration
Program on Women
Northwestern University
1902 Sheridan Road
Evanston, IL 60201

A 190-page book providing overview of more than 100 careers in the health sciences, health professions, paraprofessions, and public-health fields, with instructions for career planning and exploration, information on education and training. Needs of re-entry women are discussed through-out. Compiled by Program for Women in Health Sciences, University of
California, San Francisco. $7.50.

Women in Science and Engineering: Why Not?
Women in Science and Engineering (WISE)
School of Engineering and Computer Science
California State University
18111 Nordhoff Street
Northridge, CA 91324

Describes careers in biology, chemistry, computer science, engineering, mathematics, and physics; special section for the returning mature woman student. $.35.

Women's Career Handbook
Regional Learning Service
405 Oak Street
Syracuse, NY 13203

Information gathered from participants in a local women's career workshop (plus reference sources) on specific jobs, education or training required, approximate cost of education, career outlook, salary range, skills, and duties involved. Careers include armed forces, attorney, bank manager, construction trades, health services, human services, police officer, public relations, real estate, sales, telephone crafts, TV news reporter, underwriter, and visual and performing-arts administration. Free.

Further resources, courtesy of the Ellen Morse Tishman Memorial Seminars, Hunter College

Accounting *(A Career as a Certified Public Accountant)*, American Institute of Certified Public Accountants, 666 Fifth Avenue, New York, NY 10019

Advertising *(Career Opportunities in Advertising)*, Public Affairs, American Association of Advertising Agencies, Inc., 200 Park Avenue, New York 10017

Aerospace Engineer *(Your Career as an Aerospace Engineer)*, Public Affairs Office, American Institute of Aeronautics and Astronautics, 1290 Avenue of the Americas, New York, NY 10019

Agriculture *(Rewarding Careers in a Dynamic Industry—Agriculture)*, Dean of School of Agriculture at the land-grant college or university in each state

Agronomy *(Careers in Agronomy, Crop Science, and Soil Science)*, The American Society of Agronomy, 677 South Segoe Road, Madison, WI 53711

Archaeology *(Archaeology as a Career)*, Archaeological Institute of America, 260 West Broadway, New York, NY 10013

Art *(Your Career in Art)*, Department of Public Information,

Philadelphia College of Art, Broad and Pine Streets, Philadelphia, PA 19102

Astronomy *(A Career in Astronomy),* American Astronomical Society, 211 Fitz Randolph Road, Princeton, NJ 08540

Atomic Science *(Careers in Atomic Energy),* U. S. Atomic Energy Commission, P.O. Box 62, Oak Ridge, TN 37830

Automobile Industry, Public Relations Staff, General Motors Building, 3044 West Grand Boulevard, Detroit, MI 48202

Banking *(Banking: A Career for Today and Tomorrow),* (finance, insurance, real estate, managers and officials), Banking Education Committee, The American Bankers' Association, 90 Park Avenue, New York, NY 10016

Biochemistry *(Careers in Biochemistry),* one free copy, American Society of Biological Chemists, 6950 Wisconsin Avenue NW, Washington, DC 20014

Biology *(Careers in Biology),* American Institute of Biological Sciences, 3900 Wisconsin Avenue NW, Washington, DC 20016

Botany *(Botany as a Profession),* Office of the Secretary, Botanical Society of America, Department of Botany, Indiana University, Bloomington, IN 47401

Business *(Careers in Business),* (salesmen and salespersons, commodities), Public Relations Department, Rochester Institute of Technology, P.O. Box 3404, Rochester, NY 14614

Cartooning *(A Career for You in the Comics),* Newspaper Comics Council, 260 Madison Avenue, NY 10016

Ceramics *(For Career Opportunities Explore the Wonder World of Ceramics),* Business Manager, The American Ceramic Society, 4055 North High Street, Columbus, OH 43214

Chemistry *(Careers Ahead in the Chemical Industry),* Manufacturing Chemists Association, 1825 Connecticut Avenue NW, Washington, DC 20009

Civil Engineering *(Your Future in Civil Engineering),* DOT 005 (civil engineering occupations), American Society of Civil Engineers, 345 East 47th Street, New York, NY 10017

Civil Service *(Futures in the Federal Government—Civil Service),* U. S. Civil Service Commission, Washington, DC 20415

Conservation *(A Wildlife Conservation Career for You),* The Wildlife Society, Suite S-176, 3900 Wisconsin Avenue NW, Washington, DC 20016

Construction *(Construction: A Man's Work?),* DOT 005.081, 8 (structural occupations), Assistant Director of Education, General Building Contractors' Association, Inc., Suite 1212, 2 Penn Center Plaza, Philadelphia, PA 19102

Consumer Finance *(Your Future in Consumer Finance),* Educational Services Division, National Consumer Finance Association, 1000 16 Street NW, Washington, DC 20036

Dental Assistant *(Something New in White—Dental Assistant),* Division of Dental Health, 8120 Woodmont Avenue, Bethesda, MD 20014

Dental Hygienist *(Careers in Dental Hygiene),* Division of Educational Services, American Dental Hygienists' Association, 211 East Chicago Avenue, Chicago, IL 60611

Dental Lab Technician *(Hands that Think—A Word About Careers in Modern Dental Laboratory Technology),* National Board for Certification, 210 Thomas House, 1330 Massachusetts Avenue NW, Washington, DC 20005

Dentistry *(Careers in Dentistry),* Council on Dental Education, American Dental Association, 211 East Chicago Avenue, Chicago, IL 60611

Dietetics *(Dietitians in Demand),* Public Relations Director, The American Dietetic Association, 620 North Michigan Avenue, Chicago, IL 60611

Draftsman *(Can I Be a Draftsman?),* Public Relations Staff, General Motors Building, 3044 West Grand Boulevard, Detroit, MI 48202

Electronics *(Planning a Career in Electronics),* Electronic Industries Association, 2001 Eye Street NW, Washington, DC 20006

Engineering *(A Career of Opportunity),* National Society of Professional Engineers, 2029 K Street NW, Washington, DC 20006

Engineering Technology *(Engineering Technology Careers),* National Council of Technical Schools, 1507 M Street NW, Washington, DC 20005

Entomology *(Entomology—An Exciting Scientific Career),* Entomological Society of America, 4603 Calvert Road, College Park, MD 20740

Fire Protection Engineering *(Careers in Fire Protection Engineering).* Society of Fire Protection Engineers, 60 Batterymarch Street, Boston, MA 02110

Food Processing and Technology *(The Science and Technology of Food),* Institute of Food Technologists, Suite 2120, 221 North LaSalle Street, Chicago, IL 60611

Geography *(Geography as a Professional Field),* Association of American Geographers, 1146 16 Street NW, Washington, DC 20036

Geology *(Geology: Science and Profession),* American Geological Institute, Publications Office, 2201 M Street NW, Washington, DC 20037

Graphics *(Careers in Graphic Communications),* (occupations in graphic art work), Educational Council of the Graphic Art Industry, Inc., 4615 Forbes Avenue, Pittsburgh, PA 15213

Horticulture *(Horticulture: A Rewarding Career),* American Society for Horticulture Science, P. O. Box 109, St. Joseph, MI 49085

Hospital Fields *(Your Career Opportunities in Hospitals),* Pfizer Laboratories, Public Relations Department, 235 East 42nd Street, New York, NY 10017

Hotel and Motel *(Your Career in the Hotel and Motel Industry),* The Educational Institute, American Hotel and Motel Association, 221 West 57th Street, New York, NY 10019

Insurance *(Careers in Insurance),* Insurance Information Institute, 110 William Street, New York, NY 10038

Jewelry *(The Golden Touch),* Director of Affiliate Services, Retail Jewelers of America, Inc., 1025 Vermont Avenue NW, Washington, DC 20005

Journalism *(Your Future in Daily Newspapers),* American Newspaper Publishers Association, 750 Third Avenue, New York, NY 10017

Landscaping *(Career Opportunities in the Nursery Industry),* American Association of Nurserymen, Inc., 835 Souther Building, Washington, DC 20005

Law *(The Profession of Law),* American Bar Association, Information Service, 1155 East 60th Street, Chicago, IL 60637

Library *(Future Unlimited—What You Need to Be a Librarian),* American Library Association, Office of Recruitment, 50 East Huron Street, Chicago, IL 60611

Management *(Invitation to Achievement—Your Career in Management),* American Management Association, 135 West 50th Street, New York, NY 10020

Mathematician *(Can I Be a Mathematician?),* Public Relations Staff, General Motors Building, 3044 West Grand Boulevard, Detroit, MI 48202

Mechanics and Repair Work *(Can I Be a Craftsman?),* Public Relations Staff, General Motors Building, 3044 West Grand Boulevard, Detroit, MI 48202

Mechanics and Repair Work *(Your Future in Air Conditioning and Refrigerator Engineering),* DOT 007.081, three free copies. Request bulk rate. Education Committee of

the American Society of Heating, Refrigerating and Air Conditioning Engineers, 345 East 47th Street, New York, NY 10017

Medical and Allied Fields *(Horizons Unlimited),* American Medical Association, 535 North Dearborn Street, Chicago, IL 60610

Medical Assistant *(Winning Ways with Patients),* American Medical Association, 535 North Dearborn Street, Chicago, IL 60610

Medical Librarian *(Medical Library Careers),* Executive Secretary, Medical Library Association, Inc., 919 North Michigan Avenue, Chicago, IL 60611

Medical Technology *(What Kind of Career Could I Have in a Medical Lab?),* Medical Technology, Muncie, IN 47302

Metallurgy *(Careers in Metallurgy and Metallurgical Engineering),* The Metallurgical Society of AIME, 345 East 47th Street, New York, NY 10017

Meteorology *(The Challenge of Meteorology),* American Meteorological Society, 45 Beacon Street, Boston, MA 02108

Microbiology *(Microbiology in Your Future),* The American Society for Microbiology, 1913 Eye Street NW, Washington, DC 20006

Military Service *(Basic Facts About Military Service),* Director, Department of Defense, High School News, Inc., Building 1-B, Great Lakes, IL 60088

Music *(Careers in Music),* Executive Secretary, National Association of Schools of Music, 1424 16th Street NW, Washington, DC 20036

Nursing *(Do You Want to Be a Nurse?)*, Committee on Careers, National League for Nursing, 10 Columbus Circle, New York, NY 10019

Occupational Therapy *(Occupational Therapy Handbook)*, American Occupational Therapy Association, 251 Park Avenue South, New York, NY 10010

Office Worker *(Can I Be an Office Worker?)*, Public Relations Staff, General Motors Building, 3044 West Grand Boulevard, Detroit, MI 48202

Optometry *(Optometry: A Career with Vision)*, American Optometric Association, 7000 Chippewa Street, St. Louis, MO 63119

Parole and Probation *(Careers in the Criminal Justice System)*, NCCD Information Center Librarian, National Council on Crime and Delinquency, 44 East 23rd Street, New York, NY 10010

Personnel Work *(Your Career in Public Personnel Administration)*, Public Personnel Association, 1313 East 10th Street, Chicago, IL 60650

Pharmacology *(A Career in Pharmacology)*, American Society for Pharmacology and Experimental Therapeutics, Inc., 9650 Rockville Pike, Bethesda, MD 20014

Pharmacy *(See Your Future in Pharmacy)*, American Pharmaceutical Association, 2215 Constitution Avenue NW, Washington, DC 20037

Physics *(Physics as a Career)*, American Institute of Physics, 335 East 45th Street, New York, NY 10017

Physiology *(Consider Physiology)*, DOT 041.081, American Physiological Society, 9650 Rockville Pike, Bethesda, MD 20014

Podiatry *(Students—Consider a Career in Podiatry)*, Director of Public Affairs, American Podiatry Association, 20 Chevy Chase Circle NW, Washington, DC 20015

Psychiatry *(Careers in Psychiatry)*, Roche Laboratories, Division of Hoffman-La Roche, Inc., Nutley, NJ 07110

Psychology *(A Career in Psychology)*, American Psychological Association, 1200 17th Street NW, Washington, DC 20036

Public Relations *(An Occupational Guide to Public Relations)*, Public Relations Society of America, Inc., 845 Third Avenue, New York, NY 10022

Radio *(Careers in Radio)*, National Association of Broadcasters, 1771 N Street NW, Washington, DC 20036

Recreation *(The Future Is Yours in Parks and Recreation)*, National Recreation and Park Association, Professional Development Service, 1700 Pennsylvania Avenue NW, Washington, DC 20006

Retailing *(Careers in Retailing)*, Public Relations Department, Rochester Institute of Technology, P.O. Box 3404, Rochester, NY 14614

Secretary *(You as a Secretary)*, School Department, Royal Typewriters, 150 New Park Avenue, Hartford, CT 06106

Social Work *(Twenty Questions and Answers About Social Work)*,

National Commission for Social
Work Careers, 2 Park Avenue,
New York, NY 10016

Sociology *(A Career in Sociology)*,
The American Sociological
Association, 1001 Connecticut
Avenue NW, Washington, DC
20036

Speech and Hearing *(Speech
Pathology and Audiology)*,
American Speech and Hearing
Association, 9030 Old Georgetown
Road, Washington, DC 20014

Statistics *(Careers in Statistics)*,
American Statistical Association,
810 18th Street NW, Washington,
DC 20006

Teaching *(Invitation to Teaching)*,
Association for Childhood
Education International, 3615
Wisconsin Avenue NW,
Washington, DC 20016

Teaching *(Jewish Education Needs
You—Make It Your Career)*,
American Association for Jewish
Education, 101 Fifth Avenue,
New York, NY 10003

Telephone Industry *(Employment
Outlook in Telephone
Occupations)*, Communications
Workers of America, 1808 Adams
Mill Road NW, Washington, DC
20009

Television *(Careers in Television)*,
National Association of
Broadcasters, 1771 N Street NW,
Washington, DC 20036

Transportation *(Opportunities in the
Trucking Industry)*, Public
Relations Department, Education
Section, American Trucking
Association Inc., 1616 P Street
NW, Washington DC 20036

Typography *(A Career in
Typography Today)*, International
Typographic Composition
Association, Inc., 2233 Wisconsin
Avenue NW, Washington, DC
20007

Veterinary Medicine *(Dimensions of
Veterinary Medicine)*, American
Veterinary Medical Association,
600 South Michigan Avenue,
Chicago, IL 60605

X-Ray Technology *(The Challenge—
Radiologic Technology)*, The
American Society of Radiologic
Technologists, 645 North
Michigan Avenue, Chicago, IL
60611

F. Suggestions for Further Reading

Abarbanel, Karin, and Siegel, Connie. *Woman's Work Book* New York:Praeger, 1975.

Bernard, Jesse. *The Future of Motherhood.* New York: Penguin, 1975.

Bolles, Richard. *What Color Is Your Parachute?* Berkeley, Calif: Ten Speed Press, 1972.

Fader, Shirley Sloan. *From Kitchen to Career.* New York: Stein & Day, 1977.

Jessup, Claudia, and Chipps, Genie. *The Woman's Guide to Starting a Business.* New York: Holt, Rinehart & Winston, 1976.

Lederer, Muriel. *Blue-Collar Jobs.* New York: Dutton, 1978.

Lembeck, Ruth. *Job Ideas for Today's Woman.* Garden City, N.Y.: Dolphin, 1975.

Loeser, Herta. *Women, Work, and Volunteering.* Boston, Mass.: Beacon Press, 1974.

Mathews, Kathy. *On Your Own: 99 Alternatives to a 9–5 Job.* New York: Vintage Books, 1977.

Medley, H. Anthony. *Sweaty Palms: The Neglected Art of Being Interviewed.* Belmont, Calif.: Lifetime Learning Publications, 1978.

Mitchell, Joyce Slayton. *I Can Be Anything.* New York: Bantam, 1978.

Nash, Katherine. *How to Find Your "Career Success Pattern," Get the Best of Yourself!* New York: Grosset & Dunlap, 1976.

Robbins, Paula. *Successful Midlife Career Change.* New York: Amacom, 1978.

Robertson, Jason. *How to Win in a Job Interview.* Englewood Cliffs, N.J.: Prentice-Hall, 1978.

Schwartz, Felice et al. *How to Go to Work When Your Husband Is Against It, Your Children Aren't Old Enough, and There's Nothing You Can Do Anyhow.* New York: Simon & Schuster, Catalyst, 1972.

Sheehy, Gail. *Passages.* New York: Dutton, 1976.

Spauer, Sarah. *Non-Traditional Careers for Women.* New York: Julian Messner, 1973.